THE MEXICAN SOLDIER

1837-1847
ORGANIZATION, DRESS & EQUIPMENT

BY JOSEPH HEFTER

Edited & Expanded By
Patrick R. Wilson

Flag Illustrations
By Eric Cox

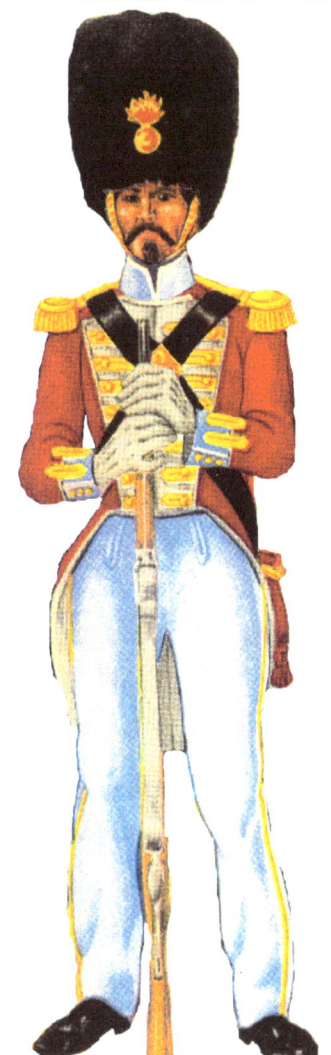

The Mexican Soldier, 1837—1847
By Joseph Hefter

Contents Coypright ©2008, ©2013 by
The Virtual Armchair General
(Portions credited to the original owners
or Copyright holders)
10208 Haverhill Place, Oklahoma City, OK 73120-3922

To View Other Titles And Products, Please Visit
www.thevirtualarmchairgeneral.com
Address Comments to TVAG@att.net

First Printing, April, 2008
2nd Printing (Revised), October 2009
3rd Edition Jan, 2014

TABLE OF CONTENTS

Section	Page	Section	Page
Introduction to The Third Edition/ Editor's Introduction to the 50th Anniversary Edition	3	**1839**	47
Original Introduction/ The Mexican Army Prior to 1837	5	**Table: Infantry Reorganization of March 16, 1839**	48
Officers Dress, Rank Insignia	6	**Table: Cavalry Reorganization of March 16, 1839/Table: Infantry Uniform Color Regulations of July 10, 1839**	49
Dress Regulations, 1832	7	**Table: Cavalry Uniform Color Regulations of July 10, 1839/*Azul Turqui***	50
Soldiers: The Men, Their Pay, Health & Discipline	8	**The Light Mounted Regiment of Mexico/ The Active Commerce Regiment of Mexico**	51
Weaponry	11	**The New Uniform Regulations of 1840/ Officers Dress**	52
Table: Inventory of Fire & Edged Weapons, November, 1839	12	**Infantry Dress**	53
Tactics, Bugle Calls	13	**Cavalry Dress/Artillery Dress/ Engineers Dress**	54
Sheet Music—Bugle Calls of the Mexican Army	14	**The Battalion of Invalids of Mexico/ Retirees/ The First Active Regiment of Mexico/1841: The Reversal of the Regulations of 1840/ 11th Infantry & 9th Cavalry/ The Tulancingo Cuirassiers/ The Grenadier Guards**	55
Cavalry Arms & Equipment	15	**1842**	56
Cavalry Drill	16	**7th Cavalry/Marines/The "Fixed" Units**	57
Presidial Companies/ The Military Health Corps	17	**1843/ The Jalisco Lancers/ The Mounted Rifles (*Cazadores*)/ The Standing Battalion of Mexico/ Hussars of the Guard/1845**	58
The Military College	20	**The 1st Cavalry/1846 4th Light Infantry/1847**	59
Military Headgear	21	**Identifying Uniform Components**	61
New Regulations & New Units, Year By Year/1835	22	**Tables: Battle Record of the Mexican Army**	63
Table: Army Reorganization of December, 1835/Active Commerce Regiment of Mexico/1836	45	**Chronology of Government Changes, 1836-1848**	65
1837/1838	46	**The Roll of Honor**	66

COLOR PLATES EXTEND FROM PAGES 23 THROUGH 44

Introduction To The 3rd Edition

This edition of *The Mexican Soldier* represents an attempt to make a remarkable work of history and art more widely available than the two previous editions. Re-published privately by this Editor and sold through his niche imprint, The (Virtual) Armchair General Publishing, almost six years ago, the book has been primarily available to war game hobbyists and some historians. Yet, with the continuing "democratization" of publishing, it has become practical to re-introduce it to mainstream booksellers and libraries, and still in a presentation befitting its subject matter and significance.

For the reader discovering (or re-discovering) Joseph Hefter's seminal work in this Edition, full background information on its return may be found in the original Introduction, below. However, it should be noted that while the text remains solely the author's own, the captions to the extra illustrations, as well as footnotes, were added by the Editor in order to help clarify a few points or add extra information.

It is still the Editor's/Publisher's hope to expand this volume—if not produce a separate companion work—reproducing more of Hefter's other works on the Mexican Army, particularly regarding the Texican Revolt of 1836, the Army/Navy of The Republic of Texas, *Soldadera's* serving with the Mexican Army, and more, in the period leading up to the Mexican-American War of 1846. Any parties with copies of such surviving works are still encouraged to make contact me via the E-mail address appearing beneath the Frontispiece.

Finally, I wish to repeat my thanks to the original Subscribers listed on The Role of Honor at the end of the book who made this work possible. And to those for whom *The Mexican Soldier* is "new," I believe I can promise a remarkably good read and an invaluable resource for years to come.

Patrick R. Wilson,
December 15th, 2013

Editor's Introduction To The 50th Anniversary Edition

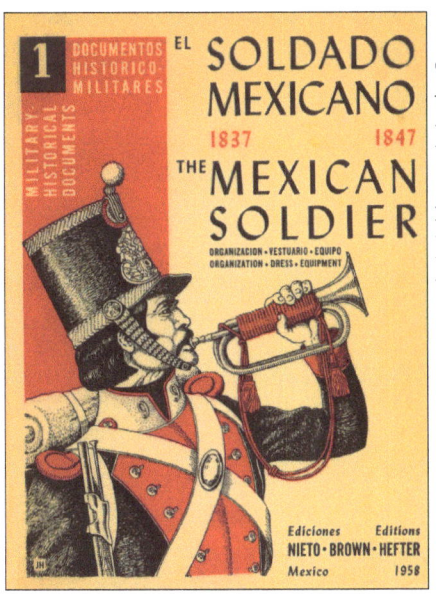

Artist and historian, Joseph Hefter, with the aid of several colleagues, created in 1958 what is still considered the "Last Word" on the appearance, equipage, and organization of the Mexican Army from Independence through the Mexican-American War.

The sources available to Mr. Hefter *et al* were the original official military records, or at least such as had survived that war and more of Mexico's tumultuous 19th and early 20th Century invasions and civil wars. This degree of accessibility has not been equaled in the years since and his book, privately published only in limited numbers, quickly became the indispensable—almost legendary—guide. It seems that every English language book written since then about the Mexican-American War of 1846-48 has relied heavily on Hefter's work. Indeed, many of the same passages have been paraphrased or just copied verbatim by successive authors.

As the years have passed, this small volume has grown harder and harder to find, and surviving copies are showing the effects of the half-century since the only printing.

Among the various hats this Editor wears, one is that of a war games rules designer on historical subjects, and as such it is imperative to find the most complete and useful information possible in order to get not only the bare facts, but the all important "feel" for a period or event. So far as the Mexican War goes, I was fortunate to have acquired an original copy of *The Mexican Soldier* some 25 years ago, but only recently have I finally been able to make full use of it.

As I have encountered sources by other authors working since 1958, and corresponded with aficionados of the subject, it became apparent that while most of them had at least heard of "Hefter," very few had actually been able to consult the work directly. Only rarely does a battered copy appear among the rare book listings, and—understandably—libraries tend not to allow their copies to leave the premises. Indeed, the original books, printed digest size on pulp paper with a light card cover, have not fared well with the years.

Eventually, I resolved that this remarkable work should return to new generations of historians, re-enactors, war-gamers, illustrators, miniaturist sculptors, and uniform buffs. After exercising due diligence in researching the history of the work, it became apparent that the original Copyright had lapsed after Mr. Hefter's death in 1978, and consequently I have taken the opportunity to republish in this the 50th Anniversary of its original printing, and the 160th of the end of the Mexican War.

The original text followed a loosely chronological presentation of developments and regulations, as Hefter explains in his Introduction. Unfortunately, this made looking for information on specific subjects (e.g. infantry organization, tactics, or details of specific units, etc) very much a "needle/haystack" operation. Consequently, I have exercised my Editor's prerogative and conducted an extensive rearrangement. Now there are sections on Organization, Weaponry, Tactics, Health Corps, and other Services, followed by a nearly year-by-year record of changes and developments. Largely due to the Editor's limited command of the Spanish language, it was decided to forego the original duplicated text (Spanish and English) in favor of an "all English" presentation.

Otherwise, exactly one word of Mr. Hefter's text has been changed, though a number of typographical and other minor (but confusing) errors have been corrected.

Originally, eight color uniform plates graced the book's pages, and these have all been enlarged and restored to something like their original brilliance.

Another eight pages of uniform plates and diagrams were printed in black-and-white, possibly from sheer economic necessity as the Author and his colleagues printed the work at their own expense. All but one of these have now been "colorized" for this new edition based entirely on information in the text. Three more of Hefter's uniform plates have been added from a history of the San Blas Battalion.

One of the more esoteric features of the original work was a page of sheet music with a number of basic Bugle Calls of the Mexican Army. With the aid of Dr. John P. S. Wilson, this dark, cramped page has been made legible, and some apparent earlier transcription errors corrected.

New illustrations by Hefter originally appearing elsewhere of weapons and accoutrements have been added in order to present a more comprehensive picture in keeping with the original work's theme.

To round out the work, Mr. Eric Cox has designed a selection of illustrations of Mexican Army Flags specifically for this work. In the original booklet, only one Cavalry Standard appeared. In order to fill this otherwise glaring gap in coverage, the new examples were created from rare photos collected in our researches. In this regard, I wish to thank Dr. Eliseo Vilalta Perdomo of the Technológico de Monterrey, Campus Irapuato, who provided invaluable flag resources not otherwise available in the U.S. Similarly, Anton Adams, author of *The War In Mexico* (The Emperor's Press, 1998) generously shared his own flag and other materials, including further examples of Mr. Hefter's art.

Special thanks must go to Mr. David M. Sullivan, Administrator of the Company of Military Historians, for permission to reproduce the plate of *Colegio Militar* uniforms which appeared in *Military Uniforms in America: Years of Growth, 1796-1851*. Mr. Mike Koury of The Old Army Press graciously gave permission to use some of Mr. Hefter's line drawings not seen in many years.

Hefter's painting "Mexican Sergeant, Matamoros Battalion in Texas, 1836," which appears on the back cover, was commissioned by author Jerry Gaddy for his book *Texas In Revolt* (Old Army Press, 1973). No ownership of this image is claimed by the publisher of this work.

Finally, Ms. Annette Asprin provided crucial transcriptions which made the entire project possible.

It is my hope that by bringing back this remarkable resource, better than ever, new attention may be drawn to Joseph Hefter whose original works have vanished, and remembered by only a fortunate few. If this publication sparks new interest in his life's dedication—and the man himself—it will be a worthy success.

Patrick R. Wilson
April 10, 2008

THE MEXICAN SOLDIER 1837-1847
Military Organization, Dress, Equipment and Regulations
Compiled from Original Sources, 1958

Introduction

During the turbulent decade 1837-1847 the Mexican military establishment stood in the field against Texas, France and the United States. Passing through stages of splendor, heroics and debacles it rendered ample testimony to the high courage, endurance, loyalty and sacrifice of its rank-and-file. History is explicit in recording the words, deeds and likenesses of political and military leaders of the period, but the Mexican conscript, the fighting man, remains blurred and forgotten in the background. The pages that follow try to show in clearer relief these stoic and colorful figures so intensely interesting to military historians and researchers.

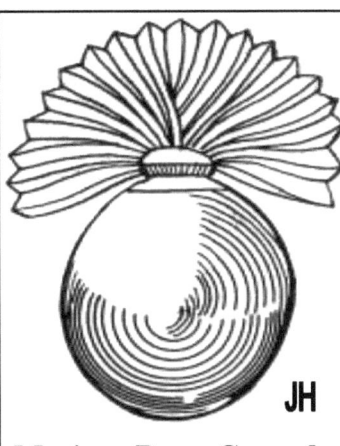

Mexican Brass Grenade from the cartridge pouch of a Grenadier in 1836; found on the San Jacinto battlefield. Property of Mr. J. Hughes. *(Illustration courtesy of the Old Army Press)*

Authentic pictorial material on the appearance of the Mexican soldier throughout this decade is exceptionally meager. The Military Historical Archives at the Defense Ministry contain carefully catalogued original manuscripts and printed text on the dress, equipment, armament and accoutrements of that time, but the drawings that accompanied uniform decrees, regulations and contracts are no longer available; the Army Library possesses documents with some sketchy military figures dating back to this tragic epoch; the Museum of History at Chapultepec Castle and the Churubusco Convent conserves valuable portraits, paintings, prints and isolated fragments of uniforms, weapons and insignia, but an adequate iconographic summary that could give tangible shape to the somber drama of these ten years does not exist.

This monograph condenses its documentary information in chronological order. Wording of military laws and ordinances, illustration of uniform, arms and equipment follow the original texts, objects, relics, paintings and prints as closely as possible. Without claiming to be the final word on this subject, the text and plates attempt a systematic reconstruction of a visual image of the Mexican military units a hundred and twenty and a hundred and ten years ago.

The contents could not have been brought together were it not for the unselfish co-operation of military historians General Ruben Garcia Velazquez de Leon, the late General J. Domingo Ramirez Garrido, and Lieutenant Colonel Alberto Guerra y Portugal of the Mexican Army, the participation of Mrs. John Nicholas Brown, the technical assistance of Mrs. Angelina Nieto, and the research, illustration and editorial work of Mr. J. Hefter.

The Mexican Army Prior to 1837

On July 14th 1832, a clash at Anahuac initiated three years of preliminary conflict between American settlers and small Mexican Army detachments in Texas.

At the time of the first major skirmishes at Gonzalez, Concepcion and Bejar, October to December 1835, the Mexican Army had theoretical Battalions and Regiments where in reality squads or picket-guards only existed. Before 1835 was over, six thousand raw recruits were hurriedly raised, armed and equipped for the 1000 mile march from San Luis Potosí across the northern deserts. After two months of cold and hunger, abandoned corpses and vehicles marking their route, the remnants of this improvised force reached and occupied San Antonio in February and captured Fort Alamo in March, 1836.

This was the nucleus that later developed into the Mexican field army. Its principal leaders and organizers were former Spanish officers. Santa Anna enlisted as a cadet in the royal Standing Regiment of Vera Cruz and rose to Colonel. Filisola distinguished himself in the King's service in Spain and New Spain. Bustamante started as lieutenant in the Spanish San Luis Regiment, similarly did Paredes, Armijo,

Dominguez, Canalizo, Cortazar, Barragan, Amador, Vazquez, Ceballos and others. Under their influence the Spanish pattern prevailed in tactics, ordinances, uniform, armament and drill, so that the Mexican officer and soldier of this period looked picturesque but somewhat outmoded.

The organic and physical reconstruction of the Mexican serviceman in the 1830's can be attempted with limitations only. Troops frequently had to be raised by arbitrary methods, organized and equipped in a hurry without funds, under trying conditions of procurement and supply. Systematic records were seldom kept and repeatedly lost or destroyed. As late as 1851, the Army General Staff noted that "…The premises of the General Headquarters Secretariat being occupied by the U.S. forces, its archives suffered general confusion… all files were found mixed up and mutilated; as a result there are some mistakes in the decrees…" Solid documentary and pictorial evidence is still too scarce and fragmentary for this period.

The Mexican generals' and senior officers' corps consisted of veterans of the colonial army and of the War of Independence as well as of numerous new political and social appointees. In a memorial to the Chamber of Deputies on April 11, 1834, the Secretary of State and of the War Office criticized the "…Prodigality of ranks and decorations conferred on a multitude that does not know how to lead … as a result of this disorder, well trained and punctilious officers have retired from the service…," a statement that struck home glaringly on the battlefields of Texas and of Mexico. Many staff grades and subalterns, however, left a fine record of bravery and discipline under fire.

Officers' Dress

Officers were colorfully attired. The Generals' gala dress was reformed Aug. 10 1831 but retained 1823 and 1827 features. It consisted of a dark blue tailcoat with red collar, cuffs, lapels, lining, bars and piping, horizontal pocket flaps with 3 buttons, gold epaulettes in raised leaf-work with an embroidered metallic silver eagle and heavy bullion fringes. Cuffs, collar and lapels were edged with a 1" wide gold embroidery of interlaced palm, laurel and olive leaves. No definite design was followed; simple narrow borders were used alongside of elaborate fantasies employing scrolls, flowers, bands and quivers. Division Generals wore two rows of this embroidery on cuffs and lapels, and one on collar. Brigadier Generals had only one row on cuffs, lapels and collar.

The Division General wound a sky blue silk sash around the waist, with two knots above the metallic gold fringes showing the same embroidery as on cuffs, and the Brigadier General a dark green sash with one knot. White trousers worn over the boot shafts were for gala, and blue or grey ones for service. The hats were black fore-and-aft bicorns edged with gold lace and topped with three loose plumes in the national colors over a tricolor cockade (PL. I-a).

Except in line of duty, Generals were free to wear overcoats, frock coats or fracs, but always with their respective sashes traversed with the embroidery of their rank. A black vest was worn for official mourning. Generals who held active command as Colonels since the War of Independence could, at their option, wear the Colonel's uniform of their erstwhile branch—Infantry, Cavalry, Artillery, Engineers or Navy—with their last unit number embroidered on collar, but displaying General's epaulettes, sash and cuff embroidery.

Officers and noncoms wore the same dress as the rank and file, of finer materials and with insignia of Jan. 18, 1830, retaining some features from 1823.

Rank Insignia

In the Regular (*Permanente*) Army, Colonels wore two heavy bullion fringed epaulettes—gold for foot, silver for mounted services—with a large star in opposite color on the oval blade, and Lieutenant Colonels the same epaulettes without the stars. Both used a bright red silk waist-sash and tassels and a tricolor plume on hat. Colonels, Lieutenant Colonels and all Adjutants carried a cane, but all had to use shako or helmet when in formation with their troops.

First Adjutants wore two stiff epaulettes with smooth bullion straps and heavy fringes, held down by shoulder loops of 5-strand lace, as well as the red sash and tricolor plume.

Captains had two epaulettes of gold or silver thread with loops of the same cloth as coat, Lieutenants and Second Adjutants one such epaulette on right shoulder, Sub-lieutenants, Sub-adjutants and

Ensigns one on left shoulder.

Subalterns wore bicorns without lace or plumes when on individual assignment. The tricolor plumes were a distinction of senior combat officers and no other military personnel was permitted to wear them. First Sergeants and Cornet Majors wore two flexible silk epaulettes, crimson for Infantry, green for Cavalry, while Second Sergeants had one only on the right shoulder, all held down by shoulder loops in epaulette color without metallic admixtures.

In the Active Militia (*Activo Milicia*), Inspectors and officers used insignia opposite to the Regular Army: silver epaulette straps for Infantry and gold ones for Cavalry. Militia sergeants wore flexible epaulettes like Regular Army, but fringes in opposite colors: Infantry a crimson strap with green fringe and Cavalry a green strap with crimson fringe. Corporals apparently conserved their 1823 diagonal ½" wide linen stripe from inner seam of both cuffs to outer seams of elbows and carried a crude finger-thick flexible wooden switch to belabor the privates without doing them serious damage. The switch was an exclusive distinction of corporals and a remnant of an 18th century Spanish ordinance; only Military Academy and Invalid Corps corporals did not carry the switch as incompatible with the dignity of cadets or invalids (PL. I-c).

Dress Regulations, 1832

On Dec. 27, 1831, issuing invitations for bids on the *Dress Contract for the Army of January 2, 1832* the government stated that the dress situation "…Becomes more difficult every day because of the confusion in which it finds itself… being unable to attain that all organizations present themselves completely equipped… for which reason the former contract (of 1824) is being cancelled. The new contractor ought to manufacture the required number of Infantry and Cavalry uniforms within a reasonable period designated by the government… in accordance with models that will be presented at the time… as the dress items used by the army of today are not the same that the General Ordinance specifies…."

To speed up and simplify manufacture, the items were divided into groups of 30 and 60 month duration. The infantryman would receive, in the 30-month group: a tailcoat of Querétaro cloth* with scarlet collar, lapels and cuffs, white piping, coarse lining and yellow metal buttons; the contract does not call for cloth trousers but provides 2 sailcloth jackets and pants, 2 linen shirts, 2 (black) velveteen neckties, 2 pairs of shoes, one barracks cap with band, tassel and visor (PL. V-c).

In the 60-month group: an overcoat of Querétaro cloth with yellow metal buttons, a shako of tanned cowhide with brass plate and chinstrap, cotton cords and an elongated wool pompon, and a hide or canvas knapsack with buckskin straps, leather furniture and a canteen (PL. I-f).

For the cavalryman, the 30-month group consisted of a tailcoat of scarlet Querétaro cloth with green collar, lapels and cuffs, coarse lining and white metal buttons, a pair of Querétaro cloth riding pants with antelope skin seat lining, cordovan bells at the bottom and a cloth stripe at side seams, a pair of cloth pants with stripes for dismounted duty, sailcloth jacket and pants, 2 linen shirts, 2 velveteen neckties, 2 pair of shoes, a barracks cap same as Infantry.

In the 60-month group: a cape of Querétaro cloth with white buttons, a shabraque of same cloth with wide cotton band, 2 cotton tassels and lining of sailcloth or coarse brown linen (PL. II-b), a saddle roll of green Querétaro cloth with scarlet cover, trimmed with a cotton band, buttoned and sailcloth lined, a sailcloth or coarse brown linen grain bag, a helmet of tanned cowhide with a large brass shield, comb and chinstrap, wool plume and a crest of goat pelt. In addition, leather furniture, a bandoleer, nosebag, canteen and a pair of gloves with gauntlets (PL. I-b).

Bids covered 20 to 25 thousand uniforms divided evenly between Infantry and Cavalry, with 12 to 15 thousand to be delivered the first month.

On Jan. 27, 1832, leather furniture was specified as a tin cartridge box, buckskin cross belt with frog, canteen with strap, blanket carrier with buckles and a burlap blanket for Infantry; for Cavalry, the same cartridge box with loops for the cartridges, cross belt, waist belt and slings of buckskin, metal buckle, rings, studs and an iron hook.

* It seems the Author could not ascertain exactly what "Querétaro cloth" was, but it was apparently dark blue.
† A Mexican "foot" is equal to .926 of its English counterpart, or approximately 11⅛ inches.

Fifteen months later, in June 1833, an order changed the contract uniform to a dark blue coatee with red collar, cuffs, bars and piping, unit number embroidered on collar, dark blue or white canvas pants, and shako with yellow metal ornaments (PL. I-d).

Apparently both the 1832 contract and the 1833 regulation dress were in use until July 1839 when every Regiment received its own distinctive uniform.

Soldiers: The Men, Their Pay, Health and Discipline

The minimum height without shoes was 70 Mexican inches (reduced to 60" in June, 1839). The average soldier was of less than medium stature; service papers list heights of 5-2-4, 5-0-8, etc., in feet, inches and lines (a line approx. 1/16").†

By 1835, the soldier's pay for a month of 25 days amounted to 19 *pesos* 4 *reals* (a *real* was 1/8 of a *peso*) and 9 *granos*; by adding bed-and-light allowance, this rose to 20 *pesos*, 8 2/3 *granos* from which deductions were made for laundry 0-2-6, barber 0-1-0, shoes 0-7-0, a rifle plug 0-0-6, cigars 0-2-0, etc.

General issue per man was increased to a barracks cap, 3 shirts, a cloth tailcoat, 2 canvas jackets, a pair each of gala, cloth and canvas pants, necktie, pair of shoes, a shako with cords and ornaments, and overcoat, blanket with carrier, knapsack with straps, tool set, canteen, cross belt with cartridge box, cross belt with frog, scabbard and bayonet, fusil, satchel of trimmings and towel.

Pay rates were changed on Feb. 18, 1839. That for Generals was established as: Division General 4,000 *pesos* a year in garrison and 6,000 in field with 12 rations of bread a day, fodder and straw; Brigadier General 3,000 a year in garrison and 4,500 in field plus 9 rations a day. For serving as Commander in Chief, 150 *pesos* a month were paid extra, for commanding a Division, 60, and a Brigade 40 *pesos*.

As of May, 1839, rank-and-file pay rate pay rate for a 30-day month amounted to: First Sergeant, Grenadier Company 26 *pesos*, Rifle Company 25, Fusilier Company 14, Second Sergeant 20, Bugle Corporal 18, Bugler 17, Drummer or Fifer 14, a Pioneer Corporal of Grenadier or Rifle Companies 18, Fusilier Corporal 17, Grenadier and Rifleman private 16, Fusilier private 15 *pesos*.

Dress, equipment and armament continued scarce. In 1841, the treasury allotted 5 *reals* (0.625 *pesos*) a month as clothing allowance for every infantryman and double that for every cavalryman. Time sheet and service booklet carried in knapsack showed simple annotations such as:

Hidalgo Battalion, 2nd Company, Juan Perez Garcia native of Orizaba, Ver., 5 ft 1-1/4" high, was entered on the roll of this Company today, the date on which he enlisted voluntarily for eight years which he will complete on Dec. 15th 1842. This 15th day of December 1834. Signature of Colonel – Initials by Major – Full Signature of Captain.

On the time paper of those who did not enlist voluntarily, the phrase "…Who was assigned to armed service for ten years…" was substituted.

Toward the end of the decade, a more extensive contract was being issued. The left margin listed religion, age, marital state, trade, height, hair and brows, eyes, color of skin, nose, beard and distinguishing marks. Under the heading e.g.: "3rd Line Battalion, 1st Fusilier Company, Contract of Private Efren Hernandez" followed the text:

Before me, the Commissioner for National Military Service, there appeared a recruit who said that his name was Efren Hernandez, native of Jalisco, resident of Jojutla, son of Epigenio Hernandez and Sara Medina residing in Jojutla where they are known, having relatives in Cuautla, his personal description stated on the margin; the Nation will give him 15 pesos a month and assist him in his illnesses. If he will become disabled in service or will die in action or as a result thereof, he and his family will receive the pensions assigned them by existing laws. On fulfilling the period of 6 years, he will immediately receive his full discharge and the balance of his pay. Received a bounty of 10 pesos. He submits himself to the Ordinance and the laws read and explained to him in the presence of witnesses Sergeant Teofilo Herrera and Corp. Xavier Sanchez. He promises full and prompt obedience to his superiors, to follow his flag and to defend the Nation, even though it were necessary to give his life for it. This document will serve as full identification, without anything being valid against it in legal judgment, nor extra judicially (sic). *This Recruit Approved. Notes…*

Military discipline was generally lenient and military courtesy ceremonial and collective, salutes being rendered by presenting arms in formation. Only toward the end of the decade does obligatory individual saluting appear in an undated but probably 1847 regulation "…in the presence of a superior, if he is not under arms or in formation, the soldier stands with his hand at the shako or his hat removed; in the street, he brings the right hand up to the shield of the shako…."

Forced impressment of a great part of the army rank-and-file rounded up a night in homes, streets and public places produced understandably heavy desertions. An order of Feb. 13, 1837, states that "…Since it becomes every day more urgent to avoid the crime of desertion and to punish lawfully those unfortunate enough to incur in it, deserters must be efficiently persecuted and an award of 5 *pesos* is allowed for every one caught."

Further, a rate of values for individual arms was set at 8 *pesos* 4 *reals* for a rifle, 7 *pesos* for a *tercerole* and 12 for a pair of cavalry pistols, 2 *pesos* 4 *reals* for a short sword, 6 *pesos* for a sword-saber and 4 for a lance, to be deducted from the pay of recaptured deserters who had absconded with their arms.

For a second desertion, the culprits were sent to Vera Cruz, as service on the coasts of the hot country was often equivalent to a sentence of death. A census of the death rate taken in Vera Cruz hospitals in 1834 lists an average of 600 deaths a year from yellow fever, 140 from plain fever, 40 from cholera, 160 from consumption and diarrhea, 60 from inflammations and 150 from unidentified causes. Not only the rank-and-file, but officers and even generals were deserting and as of June 12, any officer who exceeded his furlough by one month was declared deserter.

On Aug. 5 a provision citing Spanish colonial laws of Feb. 9, 1796, and Jan. 20, 1821, gave absolute discharge from the army to all deserters caught in a state unfit for further military service.

Strange problems sometimes confronted the army. Southern contingents brought along many servicemen suffering from the spotted itch. Although the medical corps declared it not contagious, an order had to be issued Oct. 18, 1836 that "…Whether contagious or not, the afflicted, when their skin is perspiring, exhale an insufferable stench very much like the foul and disagreeable fetidity of vultures… noxious to the health of those who breathe it, and because of the revulsion this ill odor causes to the healthy, frequent brawls arise between the latter and the afflicted… the medical faculty is of the opinion that the *pintos* ought not to mingle with the healthy in military organizations…." There were also serious cases such as the one of …

Citizen Manuel Guevara, Sub-lieutenant in the 3rd Company of the local Artillery Brigade, charged with the crime of having protected the escape of prisoner Ignacio Alquisira while he was on guard duty at San Andres hospital, having left his quarters at the former Inquisition Building. I, citizen Rafael Palacios, 2nd Adjutant of the First Regular Artillery Brigade, making use of the jurisdiction that the Ordinance concedes an officer do hereby call on, cite and summon by first edict and notification by the common crier this above mentioned Guevara, appointing him the Fortress Quarters where he ought to present himself within the period or 30 days from this date to submit his defense, and in case of non-appearance within this referred term, his case will proceed and he will be sentenced for rebellion, a crime that deserves a heavier penalty than desertion and the one that caused his flight, thus compounding the first and second penalty without any further calls or summons, such being the will of the Nation. This edict to be posted and cried in public to bring it to everybody's knowledge this 1st day of October, 1834.

Among the common soldiers, desertion became widespread enough to constitute a drain on the armed forces and induced the government to issue, on April 4, 1838, a general amnesty for all Privates to Sergeants who had one or more desertions against them, provided they gave themselves up voluntarily within two months. Those who did not present themselves before this deadline and were caught, drew 8 years service in border or maritime garrisons. Persons who helped or harbored deserters were fined from 10 to 500 *pesos*; failure to pay meant forced public labor from 1 to 12 months. This proclamation was ordered read to all army units every month while the amnesty lasted.

The amnesty did not remedy the situation and Dec. 29 an elaborate *Penal Law for Deserters, Delinquents and the Vice Ridden* from sergeant inclusive down had to be passed. It divided them into classes with a complicated system of punishments for each.

A soldier who failed to appear at roll call four consecutive days was regarded as deserter; if he was missing less than 4 days, he was a delinquent. If he returned within 8 days after being entered as deserter, he became deserter 1st class, losing all the time he had served, forced to start his 6 year term of service all over again and subjected to 8 days of arrest. If he reported back voluntarily after the 8 days, he drew in addition 4 months imprisonment in barracks doing kitchen police.

If he did not report back and was caught after the 8 days, he was classified a 2nd class deserter, losing the time served, his back pay and subject to 2 months imprisonment. If a 2nd class deserter was apprehended a second time, he was sent for a 10 year stretch to Vera Cruz or another coastal garrison and if he deserted again from there, he drew a 15 year term of tropical service. Invalids who deserted lost their seniority and within the 1st class had to continue service in the Invalid Battalion for 10 more years; those of the 2nd class went for 10 years to Vera Cruz.

Artillery or Engineer Corps deserters drew a 10 year sentence and afterward standing service in coastal regions, and those who deserted from the coast were sent to serve 10 years in Naval Artillery or Marine Infantry. Delinquents were hit with 8 days arrest for 1 day's absence, 15 days for 2, and 20 days for 3.

Corporals and Sergeants who deserted for a 3rd time were busted for 2 months, imprisoned for 4 and then sent for a 6 year term to the coast. The same punishments were meted out to the vice-ridden, especially those who got drunk outside of barracks to a point where they could not stand up unaided, or who committed other excesses. Those who sold items of uniform or equipment were put on bread and water without pay until they made good the value of the items.

Servicemen who deserted a 4th time were henceforth forbidden to wear the uniform and had to dress in crude brown duck pants and shirt worn loose with a black strap around the waist and a plain cap without visor, piping or emblem, but displaying a white patch with the transgression written on it; they received only their food, a pair of shoes, one *real* a week and half a *real* every 15 days for soap to wash their shirt and trousers (PL. VII-d).

Officers from Colonel down sentenced for desertion by a war council lost their military exemptions from law, but were still subject to military justice for sedition or conspiracy, could not enter the officer class again for 4 years and were deprived of their rank. Officers who left their garrisons for one night without permit, or who were found at a distance of up to 4 leagues (approx. 16 miles) from their station without a passport, or who did not report at their destination within a prescribed time, were charged with desertion. Generals could only be so charged by decision of the Commander in Chief. Officers or soldiers who deserted in groups of 4 to 10 fell into the 2nd class, but if a group of more than 10 deserted, lots were drawn and every 10th man was shot, the others going for 8 years to the coast. In war, even first offenders drew 8 years at the coast, but those deserting in the field in front of an enemy, or from a column marching to battle, died before a firing squad, just as those who left a fortified point or camp threatened by attack or under siege.

The soldier who absconded with a rifle, carbine, *Tercerole*, saber, horse or saddle and engaged in armed assaults, robberies, sedition, mutiny or insubordination, was shot. In peace, abandoning a guard merited 4 years of fortress or public labor, in war a death sentence. Those who took to their heels in front of an enemy could be shot down on the spot. Ships' Masters who booked a soldier without discharge papers were subject to 6 years of fortress imprisonment; a recruiter for a foreign army died before a firing squad. Noncoms and soldiers who helped or covered up a desertion were imprisoned for 6 years in peace and shot in war.

To fill so many vacancies brought about by the Army Reorganization of 1839, the replacement method was tightened by law of Jan. 26. Each year, on Sept. 1st, every Department had to contribute its quota of men to the armed services. The drawing of lots took place under supervision of local judges on the last Sunday in October and the draftees entered service on Dec. 15th for a fixed term of six years. The law proclaimed that military service was a real merit and that discharged servicemen deserved preference in public or private employment. Only single men or childless widowers from 18 to 40 years, married men not living with their wives, and childless married men were subject to the draft and their names posted in public for 8 days.

Exempt from service were inmates and ex-inmates of penitentiaries, the incurably sick, deformed or amputees, demented or morons, those below the minimum height, veterans with 6 years previous service, the only sons of 60-year old parents or widows, providers for minor brothers or sisters, ordained church assistants and priests, men engaged to be married, chaplaincy aspirants registered 4 months before a draft, rectors, educators and intern students of colleges and universities inscribed 6 months before the draft, attorneys with offices, registered medical men, pharmacists with dispensaries, justices of supreme tribunals, city hall officials, chiefs of rural police, elementary school teachers and elected public employees.

Drafted citizens could substitute an able-bodied man, but if the substitute deserted, the original draftee had to report for service or be adjudged a deserter. Men not included in the draft could enter the service as volunteers.

The Mexican conscript often faced his fellow conscripts who had followed some uprising against the government. Twice in 1840, troops under Urrea and Mejia battled against Bravo, Santa Anna, Almonte and Valencia. Street skirmishes in the capital left the pavements strewn with corpses of the common soldier while Battalions from the provinces came and went to reinforce the loyal garrison or to oppose it.

Weaponry

The armament situation was poor. Before Independence, Mexico had a factory producing muskets and pistols of superior quality; the machinery still existed in 1834 but was no longer in use. The National Artillery Corps dating back to Feb. 14, 1824, had its Brigade of Horse Artillery suspended on Nov. 16, 1833, its workshops suffered interruptions for shortage of funds, artillery pieces were deteriorated, and gun cartridges in bad state.

The type of weapon represents somewhat of a mystery. Firearms were identified repeatedly as "English flintlock rifles," "New English rifles of the *de la Torre* (Tower) factory," and English *Terceroles.* There were even English brass drums.

In 1836, General Nicolas Bravo reported the equipment for his field forces in Texas as consisting of: English fusils with bayonets, ramrods and locks; rifle cartridges with powder and ball of 19 *adarmes* (1 3/16 oz); flints for rifles; 12 caliber infantry cartridges of cloth nap; and for his Mounted Artillery Company sabers with steel scabbards, English *Terceroles*, rifle cartridges with one-ounce balls, carbines, and quick-matches.

The Mexican *Military Review* Vol. 1, No 1 mentions an 1822 fusil and C.T. Brady in *Conquest of the Southwest* states that Mexicans used British Tower type smoothbore muzzle-loading flintlock muskets condemned as unserviceable by the British and sold to Mexico, probably referring to the "Brown Bess" with an accurate range of less than 100 yards and 0.752" caliber.

By courtesy of Mr. D.W. King, Hon. Librarian of the British War Office Library, more specifications are available on this important item.

It seems that the rifles and possibly also the *Terceroles* or carbines were made in London by Ezekiel Baker whose firearms were used in the British service from 1800 to 1838 when they were replaced by the Brunswick percussion rifle. Particulars listed in the *Textbook of Small Arms*, 1929, describe the flint-ignition Baker Rifle as 39 1/2" long, weight (without bayonet) 9.5 lbs, barrel length 30", caliber .615" , 7 grove rifling with 1 turn in 120", spherical soft lead 350 grain bullet with approx. muzzle velocity of 1200ft/sec., sighted to 200 yards.

In an article on *The Rifle in the British Service* Lieutenant Colonel A. Barker describes and illustrates the Baker firearm as the standard rifle for regular troops (PL. V-a, PL. VI, b) loading a 20-to-the-pound ball of .625" diameter, overall length 46", marked with a Crown, G.R. and Tower, fitted with a superior mechanism arranged to prevent the sear catching at half cock when firing. The Baker carbine of same caliber and gauge weighed 6.5 lbs, had 36" overall length with a 20" barrel and pronounced pistol grip. The sight was adjustable on rifle and fixed on carbine; both had a cheek piece on the butt. The carbine muzzle had a deep funnel to hold ball and patch while ramrod was being drawn by mounted cavalryman, the ramrod being attached by a swivel and topped by a large bead. Barrels were of stub twist, browned to show grain of metal.

A later contract model of 1806-1808 had the Baker mark on lock plate, plain iron barrel, swan neck cock and fixed back sight, was brass mounted, stocked to the muzzle, with a bayonet attachment frame brazed on at the side; the ramrod was heavy, with large head and the butt was placed between the feet for loading to force the ramrod down with both hands, a procedure at variance with Mexican rifle drill practice. The ball was slightly smaller than bore, requiring a greased leather patch.

Early Baker models carried an odd bayonet with 17" triangular blade fitted into brass handle, 21.25" overall length and weighing one pound; this was replaced later by a 23" long broad blade sword-bayonet with brass handle and guard bow, total length being 27.25". The Baker firearms continued in the British army until 1838. It is therefore probable that surplus, older or discarded models were shipped to Mexico during the 1830-1840 period, although documentary evidence in the archives of the Public Records Office in London would have to be searched for proof.

A comparison of ball dimensions seems to confirm the report that the Mexican garrison defending Churubusco succumbed because their ammunition boxes contained 1-3/16 oz ball for use in rifles bored for 0.6 oz troy or 0.8 Castilian ball. To this day, the wooden stairway to the upper story of Churubusco Convent shows large circular marks where the despaired defenders tried to force the outsize lead balls down the barrels by turning their rifles muzzle down and striking the ramrods against the stair threads.

Shortages of funds delayed payments due to contractors, so that the army could not insist on delivery of complete issues of dress and equipment.

The following inventory of hand firearms alone shows nearly 18,000 useless weapons against a little over 1,100 in serviceable order and less than 3,000 new ones.

In a dispatch of Sep. 10, 1840, General Arista reported to the Secretary of War that "…A certain Carabajal arrived from Texas with some American auxiliaries and a cargo of rifles. In their camp, they hoisted a flag with colors as shown in document Nr. 2; God and Liberty, General H.Q. in Matamoros, Army Corps of the North, the Commanding General…."

Small arms for Infantry and Cavalry obtained in 1843 included 5,000 English fusils, 3,000 *Terceroles*, 3,000 Cavalry swords, 5,800 Infantry sabers and 200 musicians' swords.

INVENTORY OF FIRE & EDGED WEAPONS, NOVEMBER, 1839

Weapons	New	In Service	Useless	Weapons	New	In Service	Useless
English Flintlock Rifles	1,274	7,272	9,349	Lance Points	600	2,938	63
Rifles of Different Manufacture	884	1,929	0	Cavalry Swords	128	53	184
Spanish Rifles	0	197	5,915	Loose Blades	195	12	129
Shotguns	0	82	276	Sabers	476	380	410
Cut-Down Guns	0	144	29	Sword-Sabers	637	1,297	68
Carbines	205	804	843	Infantry Sabers	68	0	21
Terceroles	474	827	680	Sappers' Machetes	12	0	0
Pistols	0	12	316	Artillery Machetes	0	0	1
Lances w/Shafts	516	1,459	885				

Tactics

Up to 1835, considerable studies were carried out in tactical theory.

Space requirements in open terrain were standardized. An infantryman, for example, occupied 2 paces in frontal rank or in Indian file with knapsack, a mounted cavalryman 3 paces (6 ft front and 9 ft sideways). Intervals between Battalions, columns or Regiments in battle line were set at 20 yards, between brigades 30 yards and 90 paces, between divisions 50 to 60 yards. Distance between Infantry files was 1 pace (2 ft), between Cavalry files 3 paces (6 ft). Standard speed for Infantry at a walk was 76 steps or 60 yards per minute, at double or quick step 100 steps or 80 yards, and at a run 200 steps or 155-160 yards per minute. Cavalry rates were 120 yards at a walk, 180 paces or 235 yards at a trot, and 100 tempos, or 385 yards at a gallop per minute.*

Rifle fire range was figured most effective at 170 yards, average at 270-280 yards and uncertain beyond that. A rifle aimed at an elevation of 40° carried the projectile 1,100-1,200 yards with enough force to wound.

In open encampments, field guards of 12 to 15 men were placed at 50 to 60 yards in front of every Battalion, and these sent out sentries for an equal distance. In case of attack, the sentries sounded alarm and assembled at their field guards; these in turn fell back on their Battalions while the latter immediately took up battle positions at the head of their tent line. Other guards were set up at the flanks and rear, the total occupying not less than $1/15^{th}$ part of the entire field force.

Field guards dispatched lookouts, listening posts and small patrols making continuous rounds under the guidance of officers of the guard. It would be interesting to reflect what the outcome of the battle of San Jacinto would have been if these sensible instructions of only a few months before had been followed. For lack of guards and of a timely alarm, Mexico lost Texas by surprise assault in less than sixty minutes.

Early in 1840, a manual of instruction in Light Infantry tactics was issued to make it "…More adaptable to the brave Mexican Army…" than the outdated 1814 method. The basic formation was closed order in depth prepared to deploy instantly into an extended or mixed order by threes. The Companies were trained to deploy in alternate wings and to pass from this position to formations 2, 3 and 4 deep, or to deploy by halves to the front or rear by left and right.

It was claimed that by individual instruction, Light Infantry soldiers could learn the rules in four days. They were taught to deliver rifle fire while gaining or losing ground, and to both flanks at the command "Stand to Fire!" and "Open Fire!" Each soldier assumed a comfortable position that offered cover, the first man in the rank opened fire and as he finished priming, number two of the same rank fired, and as soon as he had primed, number three, and so on. Men in the second rank had arms at the ready but did not fire until their companion had finished ramming down the charge, so that there was always one loaded rifle for every pair in the ranks or files.

The diagram PL. X-a represents men advancing from the ranks of a deployed Battalion to act as Sharpshooters. The function of light troops was to clear the way for their corps and then to follow the movements of the line units. After the battle, their task was to follow up a victory or to continue resistance after a defeat.

On Sept. 9, 1843, line Infantry tactics were simplified by adapting a manual elaborated by Captain Juan Ordonez, a HQ Staff attaché.

In 1844, Lieutenant Colonel Jose Lopez Uraga adapted to tactical use in the Mexican Army the French system of bayonet drill developed by Pinette, then tested and approved by the French war ministry in 1833 and 1836. Uraga introduced into his version some new maneuvers not contained in the Mexican manual. Individual bayonet drill was supposed to give an infantrymen more agility and confidence in his weapon; it embraced 22 basic positions (PL. XI-i to o).

Bugle Calls

Bugle calls to carry commands to where the voice did not reach were used in the Mexican Army since 1825. In 1835, the principal calls were: March, Retreat, Assemble, Disperse, Halt, Fire and Cease

---

*It should be remembered that these are Parade Ground rates. The actual field conditions of most Mexican battlefields would make these rates an ideal rather than a standard.

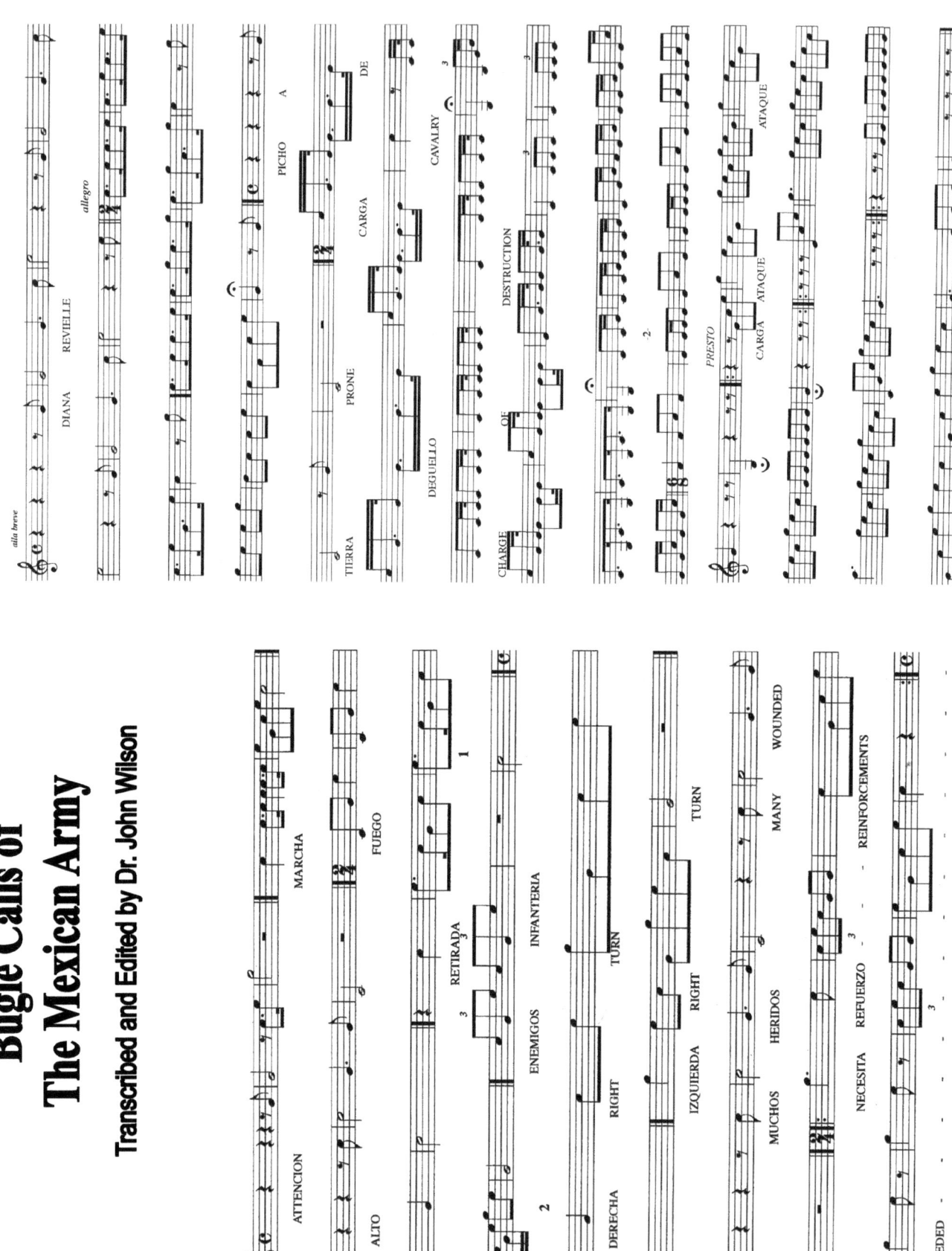

Fourteen of the 70 Infantry & Cavalry Bugle calls, with official names and numbers.
There were 57 common to both branches, 9 special Cavalry and 4 special Light Infantry calls.

Fire; when sounded, they were taken up by all bugles. "Skirmishers" or "Reunion" meant extend or contract line from point where the call sounded unless amplified by Right or Left. For Retreat, the line, reserves and skirmishers all made a left turn and retreated at the signaled pace. For "Halt," the whole line stopped, turning their front to the enemy. Assembly was always executed at the double. "Disperse" was to traverse wooded or broken terrain.

At the call "Fire" to a standing line, every man selected his target; to a marching line, single ranks were formed firing alternately; to Battalions in closed order this signal meant "Open Fire." At "Cease Fire," further discharges were suspended and the discharged rifles loaded. Other bugle signals were: Detach Skirmishers; Engage the Enemy, Pursue the Enemy; Charge or Attack (when skirmishers fixed bayonets and charged with blank arms). "Form Square" was against Cavalry attack, or forming a massed circle with fixed bayonets toward the enemy, the foremost rank kneeling and presenting arms at a slant, the butt supported against the ground and the knee (PL. X-b).

"Form the Chain" meant a line by groups of 2 to 4 sentries covering all non-fortified positions. Certain commands could also be transmitted visually by different positions of an officer's sword (PL. V-b and PL. XI-a to h).

Cavalry trumpet calls were: Saddle or General Call, Croups, Assembly, To Horse, March, Fall In, Honor Roll, Reveille or Prayer, Attention, Rest, Trot, Gallop, About Turn, To Order, Attack (or Beheading), Halt, Retreat or Tattoo. Of these calls, the *Deguello*—Beheading or Destruction—was sounded only at the culmination of a charge when 80 paces from the enemy.

At "General Call" horses were saddled and troopers made ready their gear. At "To Horse," the officers and sergeants called out all troopers, placed them in battle order at rank intervals, read the roll call and ordered to mount. In case of alarm or surprise, the "General Call" was omitted and "To Horse" sounded instead.

Cavalry Arms & Equipment

Cavalry arms were the sword or saber, carbine, pistols and lance for offense, cuirass and helmet for defense. Sword or saber hung on a sling from a waist belt and the carbine had a slide for the bandoleer hook. Dragoons used rifles somewhat shorter than Infantry, with bayonets.

Line Cavalry and Dragoons had sole-leather helmets with a bearskin crest and gilt metal chinstraps. Light Cavalry wore a cylindrical fur busby (PL. XIII-b, XIV-c), or shako with cords and chinstrap, also helmets as in PL. I-b, III-a, & XIV-b.

The lance was an important weapon and is described as 3 yards long including point and socket. The point had the form of a knife one palm (1/4 yard or 8-1/4") long with 3 or 4 cutting edges separated by concave bayonet-like gutters (Pl. VI-g), a metal crosspiece at the lower end followed by a tube and 2 iron straps a yard long to screw on to the shaft as protection against saber cuts that could lop off the point. The shaft was 1-1/2" thick, preferably of beech or nut wood with a blunt socket a palm long and hollow inside to receive the shaft. Under the crosspiece of the blade hung a 2-pointed pennant one foot long, generally red, but sometimes tri-colored (like small national flags), or in a two striped pattern, possibly in regimental colors. This served both as ornament and to scare enemy horses by fluttering in front of their eyes (PL XIII-e). At a convenient height, a leather sling was nailed to the shaft with a triple loop to suspend the lance from the right arm or as a support in swinging or thrusting; a leather tube at the right stirrup aided in resting the lance and a loop at the cinch assured that it did not fall out while maneuvering.

A blanket 10 palms long by 8 wide, and the cape or overcoat were folded into a rectangle, rolled up and strapped under the cloth or leather saddle roll 22' long by 10' wide and 5' deep for Line Cavalry and Dragoons; Hussars and mounted rifles had a cylindrical cloth roll 20" long and 6" in diameter containing cloth, canvas or leather pants, a shirt, socks, cloth and shoe brushes, a satchel with comb, scissors, pins, accessories and boot grease.

A canvas sack ½ yard wide with 2 packets contained apron and sponge; spare horseshoes were carried in a saddle pocket, and fatigue jacket and raincoat folded under the saddle roll.

Mexican military authorities copied such details freely from Spanish tactical manuals, but applied them in practice only sporadically. Reading in the last Spanish dress regulations in the Americas of Sept.

20, 1821, one recognizes numerous details that reappear in Mexican uniforms ten and twenty years later.

Cavalry Drill

In formation, the troopers were trained to call off their numbers 1 to 4 from right to left, the first, fifth and ninth man in a rank responding to Number One.

The carbine drill manual was very similar to the infantry rifle drill; in the basic position, standing or marching, the weapon rested with the barrel close to the right shoulder, ramrod to front, arm extended vertically, thumb over and index finger under the trigger guard, the rest of the fingers in back under the hammer, butt touching the trouser seam, butt point about 2" to the front of the knee (PL. III-a). On longer marches, the weapon was carried slanted against the shoulder. Loading was performed in 11 main movements or commands consisting of 18 motions called out by numbers, for example: "Prepare to Load – one two!", "Open Pan – one!," "Draw Cartridge!," "Break Cartridge!," "Close Pan!," "Cartridge in Barrel!," "Draw Ramrod!," "Ram!," "Ramrod in Place!," "Shoulder Arms!" To open fire, the command was "Prepare Arms – one – two – three!," then "Aim!" and "Fire!"

To present arms, the rifle or carbine was brought perpendicularly in front of the left eye, ramrod to front, lock at the height of the last coat button, left hand above the hammer screw, right hand around grip, thumb under the hammer and other 4 fingers against trigger guard. "Rest Your Arms!" Signified lowering the weapon until butt touched the ground at the right side of the toes, right elbow against hip and left arm loose at the side (PL. III-d). For "Brace Arms," the weapon was placed in the crook of the left arm, barrel to front, the left forearm horizontally against chest, hand open across the right breast, fingernails upward and right hand loose at the side. Other commands were "Review Arms!," "Ground Arms!," "Raise Arms!," and "Cover Arms!"

Cavalry drill also included "Hook Arms!," "Release Arms!," "Arms on Back!" (butt pointing upward), and "Unhook Arms!"

For ceremonial use, there was the position of "Render Arms!" Kneeling bareheaded on the right knee, muzzle lowered to the ground and weapon sustained in left hand resting on left thigh while the right hand held the helmet or cap upright over the flintlock. To "Funeral Arms!" the weapon was carried under the crooked left arm, butt first, the right arm detaining the barrel behind the back. "Arms at Ease!" meant carrying the weapon on either shoulder, muzzle upward, supported by one or both hands.

Delivery of fire could be speeded up by ordering "Rapid Fire—Load!," reducing the 11 loading and 4 firing movements to four groups of motions executed without waiting for the 15 individual commands. Volleys and sustained fire were performed on four orders: "Volley! First Rank!," "Prepare Arms!," "Open Fire!" At the last order, the Number One man on the right fired and reloaded; while he was priming, Number Two aimed and fired, and so in succession; after the first volley, fire was continued at will. At the call "Halt Fire!," further discharges ceased; the man who had his weapon at Prepare Arms, secured it with the right hand; those who had not yet loaded, did so and all shouldered arms.

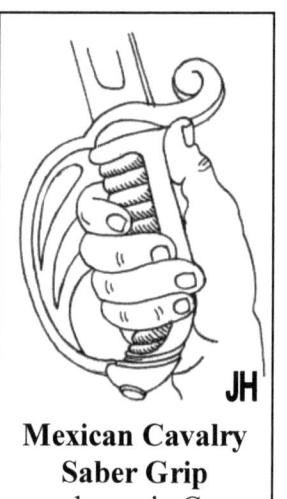

Mexican Cavalry Saber Grip as shown in Gen. Arista's drill manual, *Manejo del Sabre a Caballo*, Mexico, 1840 *(Illustration courtesy of the Old Army Press)*

Handling of the saber followed the standard pattern. The drawn sword or saber was held point straight up and cutting edge forward. At "Shoulder Saber!," blade was slanted against shoulder. For ceremonial "Render Saber!," the flat blade was lowered in right kneeling position until point touched the ground, the guard on level with bend left knee, elbow close to body, the left arm held straight down sustaining helmet or shako. At "Funeral Saber!" the blade was carried under left arm, edge down and point toward back, guard sustained by left hand.

Combat use of the saber was also standard, including the six basic cuts. Cut One from right to left traversing the adversary diagonally from left shoulder to right thigh; Cut Two the opposite of One (from left to right); Cut Three reversing Cut One from right thigh to left shoulder; Cut Four from left thigh to right shoulder; Cut Five horizontally from right to left, and Cut Six from left to right across adversary's neck. Other movements were Prepare Guard!, Guard!, Protect Left or Right!, Thrust to

Front!, Protect Bridle Arm!, Protect Sword Arm! Cut to Rear! Protect Horse Left or Right!, Cuts One—Two—and One! and other combinations, Disengage Right Front!, Thrust Right or Left against Infantry!, and the same against Cavalry.

Loading and firing of Cavalry pistols was done with the same basic movements as rifles or carbines. At "Load Pistol!" the left side pistol was drawn from the holster with the right hand receiving it in the left palm close to the hammer, barrel upward, muzzle raised over the horse's left ear, placing the right thumb on the hammer screw and closing the other fingers firmly around the weapon. Light Cavalry first folded back the front end of the shabraque before drawing the pistols.

Lancers, when dismounted in line, held the lance in the right hand at breast level between themselves and the horse's left foreleg; the lance could also be held slanted from right knee to left shoulder. At "Rest Lances!," the weapons were suspended from the crook of right arm by means of sling. "Secure Lances!" and "Prepare Lances!" meant to hold the lance perpendicularly with the hand at neck level. "Couch Lances!" for attack brought the shaft almost horizontally, 2" below right breast fixed between arm and body, thumb extended along shaft, fingers firm, lance socket in back about a foot above the croupe.

Other commands were: Lance Front!, Thrust to Left or Right against Infantry! (and the same against Cavalry), Thrust to Left or Right Rear! whereby the lance point was turned to the back while the arm was extended to the front, Cover Back!, Guard Circumference of Horse!, Disengage from Right to Rear!, and Brandish! at which the rider stood up in the stirrups, body inclined forward, raising lance to face height, socket to the left, and described an almost vertical circle down toward the back, then up the front, then above horse's head to the right and other circles in a similar manner. "Shoulder Lances!" brought the lance shaft diagonally across the right shoulder, at "Present Lances!" the lance stood vertically in front held by right arm, "Render Lances!" lowered the lance point to the ground with shaft under right arm while "Rest Lances!" planted the socket against the ground, one foot to the front.

Presidial Companies

Of the Regular Presidial Companies, 8 were stationed in Texas, 3 in New Mexico and 6 in California, all abolished Dec. 1, 1847. The uniform was the same for all except the California Companies: a coatee of shag or medium blue cloth with deep red low collar and narrow cuffs, blue pants and blue cloth cape, natural leather cartridge box and bandoleer with the *presidio* name embroidered on the latter, a black hat and black stock.

The California Companies had two uniforms: a garrison dress with dark blue tailcoat, green collar and cuffs, deep red lapels and cuff bars, white piping, dark blue pants with deep red stripes, an ornamented Cavalry shako, a shabraque of unspecified color with a white bank all around, and the initials "AC" (*Alta California*) or "BC" (*Baja California*) embroidered on the collar. Their field uniform was a dark blue round jacket with deep red collar and cuffs, grey side-buttoned chaparral pants over boots, a cowman's saddle and shabraque, round hat with white band and a dark blue cape (PL. VII-a, b, c). There were also 12 Independent Presidial Companies dressed like Regular ones.

The Military Health Corps

The common soldier's bones were not forgotten. In August 1836 a Military Health Corps was established under a Colonel as Director General, and Lieutenant Colonels as Inspectors. A Hospital Director was responsible for prompt and effective assistance to the infirm, for cleanliness at the hospitals, good condition of medicines and food. The medical officers wore a bicorn hat, a dark blue tailcoat with a low green velvet collar and a gold embroidered thistle branch. Cuff, bars and piping were crimson, and a gold Aesculap mace served as coattail clasp. Gilt buttons with eagle emblems, a blue or white vest and Regular Army insignia completed their uniform.

A network of medical care covered the whole country. In addition to the Central Military Hospital in Mexico, permanent 1st Class Hospitals existed in Vera Cruz, Tamaulipas, San Luis and Chihuahua, and 2nd Class institutions in coastal and frontier states. A 1st Class Hospital was under a Director with a salary of 800 *pesos*, a Professor, a First and a Second Practicant, and staff. Hospital administration consisted of an Accountant with 1,200 *pesos* a year, a Chaplain, Commissioner, Porter, Wardrobe Keeper and Steward.

Pay rates diminished with the importance of the hospital; in Tamaulipas, the Accountant drew 600 *pesos* and in a 2nd Class infirmary only 300, but all Chaplains received 840 regardless of the size or importance of the institution.

On Jan. 29, 1842, orders were issued to all commanding officers to visit soldiers' quarters daily and to suspend any captain in whose Company food was insufficient or not well seasoned or whose premises were damp or poorly ventilated; staff officers caught misapplying a single *peso* of army funds were to be dismissed.

On Feb. 12, 1846, the Medical Health Corps was enlarged and made part of the Regular Army. Its peace footing was an Inspector General with Brigadier General's rank and a salary of 250 *pesos* a month, a Colonel as Hospital Director, 8 Lieutenant Colonel Hospital Professors, 40 Army Surgeons with Battalion Commandant rank, 40 Captains First Adjutants, 40 Lieutenants Second Adjutants, 30 Sub-lieutenants Aspirants and an undetermined number of Medical Students.

Medical officers' dress was quite distinctive: turkish blue tailcoat and pants, the latter with gold lace stripe, collar, cuffs and bars of same color with crimson piping, gilt eagle buttons and eagle coattail clasps, black bicorn hat, a sword-saber in black patent leather scabbard with gold furnishings and sword knot.

The Inspector General's hat had a wavy gold lace edging and a white plume, horizontal crimson piping around the center of his collar with a gold embroidered row of laurel leaves above and oak leaves below it, and an indented gold tape all around the collar and cuff edges.

The Hospital Director wore the same dress but a tricolor plume on hat and a single gold embroidered row around the center of the collar, half laurel and half oak leaves. Hospital Professors wore the same, but on both sides of the collar were two imitation buttonholes with red piping, the upper one edged with gold embroidered laurel, the lower one with oak leaves, the gold tape around collar and cuffs being smooth.

Army Surgeons had only one such buttonhole at each side of collar, First Adjutants similar but their hat without lace or plume and the two buttonholes on side of collar trimmed with plain gold lace and without any tape edging on collar or cuffs, Second Adjutant same with only one buttonhole, and Aspirants without any buttonhole; all subalterns also used thin fringed tassels on their sword knots (PL. XV-o, p, q & XVI-d).

In field, hospital and garrison service, all wore turkish blue frock coat with lapels, or a military short jacket without embroidery but with crimson piping and yellow accessories, and turkish blue pants with crimson stripes.

All medics carried a black patent leather surgical cartouche box on parade, covered with red kid leather for service dress (PL. XVI-e). All used the shoulder loop insignia of their rank over crimson cloth placed horizontally from shoulder seam to collar and mounted a mixed saddle with yellow accessories. The Inspector General had a red cloth saddle blanket with 2 gold lace stripes around, and triple holster covers.

The Hospital Director wore the same but of turkish blue cloth; Professors and Surgeons turkish blue with a single lace around and double holster covers, Adjutants the same but with sky blue cloth border instead of the gold lace. Surgeons and Adjutants carried black patent leather rectangular saddle valises.

The medical officers had at their disposal an ambulance section of privates and noncoms without any special uniform but armed with an Infantry saber suspended from a fixed belt, and a lance instead of the rifle.

Stretchers were carried in pairs, one soldier carrying the front legs and a cushion on his back, and another one the rear legs and a blanket. An Algerian-Mexican model stretcher or litter, evidently following the French *litiere* and *cacolets* of the African campaign, adaptable to rough and mountain country, consisted of 2 sets of legs, 2 lances, a canvas sheet, a pillow and 2 straps to attach the stretcher parts to a soldier's back on the march and to support the stretcher when carrying it; a third soldier carried reserve legs for each stretcher. Ambulance Companies were formed in proportions of 4 ambulance men for every 100 combatants in peace, and 8 in war. Sergeants and Corporals were classified as 1st and 2nd Attendants. In additions to their standard army uniform, they wore a sailcloth frock coat for hospital and field service

(PL. XVI-e). Trained by medical officers to handle wounded and manipulate stretchers, they also formed escorts for sanitation equipment in the field or en route. On the battlefield they had a special bugle call ("Hospital") at which they assembled at the rear of the line near to the main ambulance tent with a white pennant over it, located close to General HQ. At the call "Open Fire," the Attendants assembled their stretchers while the Adjutants passed up and down the line to render assistance.

After a battle, medical officers were under the obligation to attend with the same care and eagerness both victors and vanquished, nationals and foreigners. For convoys of wounded, the Algero-Mexican litters were assembled in a reclining position to be loaded one on each side of a strong mule led by an Attendant.

As a spiritual service, each medic had to inform his patients when they were in a serious condition, so that army chaplains could aid them, prepare them to die and make out their testaments. Medics were also warned to maintain good relations with army officers but to avoid fraternization with the rank-and-file. They were responsible for vaccinating every soldier and visiting all sick every morning.

The Medical Corps took active part in all battles of the Mexican-American War. Medical activities in the field are brought closer by some of the written forms used. For Example:

Pedro Lopez, Army Medical Surgeon, in charge of the sanitation service of the sector of the south, marching to battle with a force of a thousand men, with 30 ambulance soldiers and 10 portable stretchers, needs an ambulance tent and 20 Algero-Mexican litters for the sick and wounded...," or "...In today's battle, the wounded soldiers who were found and aided are 43 in all; of these, 7 are beyond remedy of the art, 5 had to suffer amputation, 10 are grave and the rest lightly wounded. The Commandant was wounded by a rifle ball in the left leg without fracturing the bone; Captain Flores received a stab wound in the right side. Besides the wounded of our division, 17 enemy soldiers were aided and one captain whose left arm had to be amputated. Grand total 64. Mexican subalterns and soldiers 43, officers 3, enemy soldiers 17, officers 1. All sanitation officers behaved with calm and eagerness in the fulfillment of their obligations, but especially so the First Adjutant who was wounded in the arm while attending a soldier in the firing line, and the Second Adjutant who was tireless in directing the stretcher bearers under fire.

All Medical Officers had to be equipped with a prescribed list of medical instruments. Medical baggage was carried along in field boxes.

Boxes with uneven numbers contained: 7 lbs rolled bandages, 4 lbs folded bandages, compresses, thread, 6 pieces of strong thread straps; white silk, half of it formed in loops; thread, waxed and tarred; 12 one-yard fracture boards and 36 of 1/3 yard with 2 rolls of adhesive plaster; a fine washed sponge; lime chloride; 6 yard sanitary cloth; 3 tin containers, a cushion with 50 thick needles, 3 cushions with 200 pins each and 2 lbs of cotton.

Boxes with even numbers carried drugs: 1 lb Jalapa powder, 16 lbs sulphate of soda, 1 lb sennes leaves, 6 lbs castor oil, 4 ozs of emetic, 6 oz ipecacuana, 1 lb calomel, 1 oz corrosive sublimate, 8 ozs quinine sulphite and 2 lbs quinine powder, 1 lb liquid ammonia, 3 lbs bicarbonate of soda, 8 ozs camphor, 4 ozs devil's stone, 8 ozs opium extract, 3 lbs nitric salt, 4 lbs crystal lead acetate, 4 lbs gum Arabic powder, 3 lbs licorice extract, 2 lbs citric acid, 1 lb blistering plaster, 1 lb mercury plaster, 6 lbs double mercury salve, 6 ozs cantharis flakes, 6 ozs belladonna extract and 2 bottles of sodium chloride.

In 1842, the Military Health Corps changed its uniform to a dark blue tailcoat with sky blue collar and cuffs, crimson lapels and cuff bars, white piping, horizontal pocket flaps with 3 buttoned points, on collar and cuffs a gold border 1" wide showing an olive branch interlaced with an Aesculap staff, only the Director wearing a double border on cuffs.

On Feb. 6, 1843, the Medical Corps was enlarged. The dress was modified to a dark blue tailcoat with sky blue collar and cuffs, crimson cuff bars, white piping, horizontal pocket flaps with buttoned points, a gold embroidered medical emblem on collar and as coattail clasp, blue or white pants and bicorn with tricolor cockade, edged with a 1" gold lace for senior officers and velvet for subalterns, straight sword with gold sword knot for senior and crimson silk for subaltern officers, gilt buttons with medical emblem and the inscription *Military Medical Corps*.

Insignia of rank for Sub-director and Consultants were a gold embroidered row of alternating laurel and olive leaves around collar, pocket flaps and cuffs, and a double row on cuffs for Director General. First Adjutants had same insignia as Director, but only half as wide, Second Adjutants same as First but only one narrow row on cuffs, Third Adjutants a gold tape only around collar and the same embroidery on cuffs as the Second but of silver tape, the First Sub-adjutant a double row of 5-strand gold lace on cuffs, the Second a single row on cuffs but collar same as Third Adjutant.

These complicated and elaborate devices lasted only six weeks, being abolished March 21st 1843.

The Military College

Cadets of the Mexican Military Academy were organized along regulations of Nov. 18, 1833 with 3 courses of 3 years each and a total personnel not in excess of 100 divided into a Cadet Company and a Sub-lieutenant Company headed by an Infantry and a Cavalry captain as first and second in command; the Companies consisted of squads of 8 under a Cadet Corporal, each two squads under a Cadet Sergeant. Cadets wore Regular Army Infantry uniforms with a visored cap instead of the shako and the *Colegio Militar* legend on their buttons. Cadet Sergeants used the insignia of Second Sergeants, and Cadet Corporals those of army Corporals but without the wooden switch. Cadet Sub-lieutenants wore Cadet dress with their epaulette of rank on the left shoulder and could wear bicorn hats when off academy grounds.

In 1839, the Military Academy under Engineer Corps jurisdiction dressed its cadets in a turkish blue tailcoat with sky blue collar and cuffs, plain sky blue pants, and Infantry shako; inside academy grounds, a turkish blue round jacket, a dark blue barracks cap with deep red cord and a small tassel, and yellow accessories.

Then, an Ordinance of December 8, 1843 called for the following new dress for Academy Cadets: Turkish blue tailcoat and trousers, the latter of somewhat lighter hue, with crimson collar, cuffs, piping and turn back linings; a single row of gilt buttons stamped *Colegio Militar* and a block stock under the collar.

All pupils up to the rank of Cadet Sub-lieutenant had a one-inch-wide gold lace edging around collar and cuffs, and gold lace shoulder straps. The black cylindrical leather shako was the standard army model, but with a crimson top, an elongated red pompon, and a brass grenade insignia. On special occasions they carried parade swords similar to those of Regular Army officers.

For daily service on Academy grounds, they wore a medium blue frock coat with red collar and cuffs, dark blue trousers in winter and white in summer; a blue visored cap or blue barracks cap with red lace and tassel. Their black leather belting was of infantry type, with brass belt plates.

An inventory of November 18, 1846, six months after the outbreak of the war, shows the 1843 issue considerably expanded. It calls for a frock coat, trousers and barracks cap of gray cloth for all service wear within the Academy, with crimson collar, cuffs, and piping, a single row of gilt buttons and cuff flaps of the same color as the coat, with three gilt buttons at the points. Gray spats were worn over black shoes under the trousers.

For drill or fatigue duty there was a short, gray, round jacket with the above crimson facings, worn with gray or white sailcloth trousers. The Cadets who took part in the defense of Chapultepec in damp September weather wore the gray service issue.

Intended for more peaceful times, there were other items of a more colorful, ceremonial and parade nature in the Academy stores.

A band of two buglers, four drummers and a fifer wore bright green tailcoats with crimson trousers, a green carrot-shaped pompon, yellow braided silk and worsted cords suspended from the left shoulder, infantry belting, and a musician's short sword. For festive or parade occasions all shakos were adorned with gold bands around the top, as well as a set of silk and wool shako cords, red for Cadets, green for Bandsmen.

Barracks caps were of the *bonnet de police* type, of medium height, with golden yellow lace trim and tassels in 1846. Beginning in July 1846, Cadets wore fringeless counter-epaulettes instead of the former gold lace shoulder straps; Cadet Sergeants were entitled to epaulettes with yellow worsted fringe, and all wore white gloves (PL. XIX-a, b, c, d, e).

Until about 1843, their arms consisted of British "Tower" Model Muskets, lances, sabers, pistols, and a 4-pounder cannon. Eleven horses for the Cavalry and Artillery Squad completed the Academy arsenal. By 1846, Baker Carbines and some American-made rifles (cut down to the stature required of the Cadets) were replacing the earlier British firearms. The personnel was limited to two Companies of 100 Cadets each, but only some 40 Cadets were present at the fall of Chapultepec.

The Mexican Military Academy fills a heroic page in the nation's military history and deserves a much more extensive description than the limited space in this study permits. A scholarly resume of the Academy was published in 1931 by General Juan Manuel Torrea under the title *The Life of a Glorious Institution*, another one *The Military Academy* by General Miguel A. Sanchez Lamego in 1947, and a fuller history by General Adrian Cravioto Leyzaola is now in press [1958].

Military Headgear

Dress regulations, contracts and inventories of this period describe military headgear only in very general terms. Contemporary illustrations and exhibits of the disbanded Artillery Museum now conserved at the Museum of History suggest that there were nearly twenty different models of shakos, helmets, caps and hats in use during the decade.

The most typical examples are:

1) A conical shiny black leather shako about 7" tall, narrow at top, green plush, round pompon on gold red stem, a double loop of 3/16" thick silver cord over creased tricolor cockade—green center, red outer band—above a horizontally oval brass shield with *Victoria* embossed over a horizontal bugle, top cinch-band of wide golden-yellow woven lace, bottom band of woven black lace, horizontal square black leather visor with rounded points, two small yellow buttons at the temples evidently for leather chinstrap; this shako of fine quality and workmanship, identified as that of a "…Military bandsman of the 2nd third of the 19th century…" belonged more likely to a Rifle Company officer in the Victoria National Guard (*Guardia Nacional*) Battalion (PL. XV-a)

2) A dull black leather shako similar to (A) but of stovepipe form, same brass shield but with eagle under *Victoria*, deep red cylindrical velvet pompon about 6" tall by 1" round, unidentified but possibly for Grenadier Company (PL. XV-b)

3) A shiny black leather shako about 8" tall, straight stovepipe shape in profile, front view showing a slightly wider top, round red plush pompon on dark cord stem, triple gold loop of 1/8" thick cord over cockade and above a large brass bursting grenade, top cinch band reddish gold lace, bottom of golden-yellow lace, visor similar to A), chinstrap of yellow metal scales mounted on black velvet band and fastened at temples by large brass knobs with bursting grenade device; there are 13 scales at each side, each scale with 4 scallops in the wider and 3 in the narrower parts; no accessory for cord attachment is visible; this shako is identified as artillery head gear but is more likely that of a Grenadier Company officer (PL. XV-b).

4) A shako similar to B) with an ornamental yellow metal shield similar to XV-e) but with crossed cannon and grenade emblem under national arms, scale chinstrap as in c), pompon as in b), but with a tuft of thin red silk cords hanging from top; bottom cinch band of black velvet, no cord attachment device; obviously headwear of an artillery officer (PL. XV-d, g).

5) A dull black leather shako, conical toward top, about 9" tall, green plush round pompon protruding horizontally, loop and cockade over large embossed metal plate reaching from cockade to chinstrap; the narrow top cinch band is of dull black leather, the bottom band of a wide stamped copper or brass strip, scale chinstrap same as in c) but with eagle on knobs, small horizontal half-moon visor of black leather; this model represents most likely the Light Infantry and National Guard (*Guardia Nacional*) type of shako (PL. XV-f).

Plate XV-f shows the national coat of arms, a spread wing eagle with serpent under a Phrygian cap surrounded by bursting rays, laurel and oak leaves and a ribbon with *Republica Mexicana* on it; the eagle rests on a decorative semi-oval shield with black Old English CM initials in center surrounded by a wreath and by bundles of flags on both sides.

6) Shako similar in shape to e) but without pompon, wide lace bands at top and bottom of crown, a large eagle or hunting horn emblem without shield or ornaments, same chinstrap but a half-moon visor turned down at a 45° angle; appears in a series of officer figures in a 1837-1847 saber handling manual (PL. V-b; XI-a, d; XV-c).

7) A tall black leather shako as in e) with loop, cockade, round front plate and chain chinstrap all silver, a long tricolor ostrich plume in place of pompon, shown in contemporary portrait of an officer apparently of mounted Militia Artillery (PL. IX-c).

The same collection preserves interesting Cavalry headwear: a Lancer officer's helmet of 1840, surprisingly like the *Chapka* of the French Lancers of the Guard of 1855, a hemispherical black leather cap with reinforced back and sloping half-moon visor, topped by a large flat square crown on narrow square stem, both of red cloth with leather piping, a narrow silver tape around the visor, another one forming an upright triangle in back, a wide silver lace covers the joint between leather cap and cloth crown; the front is covered by a pointed silver shield with a burst of blue rays bearing a large silver Mexican eagle; at both sides of the leather cap, silver lion-head knobs are attached holding a silver chain chinstrap over a red velvet band; the left side of the mortarboard bears a bright red feather plume hanging down to the level of the eagle and attached by a tricolor cockade, while the other 3 sides have small red vent buttons inserted; the safety cord, if it ever existed, is missing (PL. XV-i).

Another helmet, somewhat dubiously identified as a Grenadier Officer's helmet of 1835, is a Cuirassier or Carabinier style headgear, its crown, comb and chinstrap entirely of brass with a leopard skin turban, an elongated tricolor pompon protruding almost horizontally from tip of comb, and a long black horsetail inserted at the back base of the comb which is heavily ornamented at sides, front and top (PL. XV -j).

Four different models of barracks or forage caps were in use: a French-Spanish type *bonnet de police*, a smaller pointed and tasseled cap, a soft-crown visored cap with cinch band, piping and tassel, and a conventional French-style kepi (PL. XV-k, l, m, n). Colors were dark blue, sky blue, red, possibly also green with distinctive color trim. Bicorn hats, too, showed different shapes, heights and decorations.

The cylindrical fur busby with colored bag, the bearskin Grenadier cap, and low conical shakos with white sun-cloth were used along with civilian wide or narrow brimmed felt or straw hats.

Accessories as important to the outward appearance as bandsmen's chevrons, gaiters, shako plumes, gorgets, kepis, colored field caps, etc, appearing in contemporary paintings and prints are neither described nor mentioned in any of the dress regulations.

New Regulations & New Units, Year By Year

1835

The year 1835 saw the creation of Commandants of Fortified Places, each with a reserve Lieutenant Colonel as Sergeant Major, and a staff of 12 officers, 4 noncoms and 9 privates. The officers dressed for gala in distinctive tailcoats of somewhat bright blue with lapels, collars and cuffs darker, buttonholes trimmed with 5-strand gold lace, a broad gold band around collar and cuffs leaving only 1/3 of them exposed, gilt eagle buttons, red piping all around tailcoat and pocket flaps, and coattail clasps in the form of gold eagles. Riding pants were blue with gold stripes, or plain white, and daily service dress lapels and pants plain blue without ornament. Black bicorn hats and swords with gilt furnishings were used on duty.

Saddles, reins and straps were black with plain silver ornaments on bridle, headstall and noseband. A small saddle blanket of blue cloth edged with plain gold lace, gold tassels at the points and fur covered holsters took the place of a shabraque (PL. II-b, c, and d).

A decree of May 5, 1824, was revived in 1835 to declare some Regular and Militia units as Light Troops with 8 Companies each, one of them a Sharpshooter Company with Grenadier pay. They used small bugles for signaling and were dressed in a medium blue tailcoat with collar, cuffs and bars of the same color, red piping and yellow metal buttons; pants were grey, shako simple and light without ornaments except a pompon and a shield with unit number or initials (PL. III-d, e). Their tactics were those of 1814 except for the bugle calls.

By December 1835 the Regular Army was reorganized in the following manner:

Plate I

A. Brigadier General, Full Dress
B. 1st Sergeant, Regular Cavalry, Contract of 1832
C. Fusilier Corporal, 3rd Regular Infantry Battalion, 1833
D. 1st Adjutant, 16th Battalion, Active Militia with Troops, Contract of 1832
E. 1st Sergeant, 9th Infantry, Active Militia, Contract of 1832
F. Knapsack, Blanket, Carrying Straps, Quart Canteen of 1832.

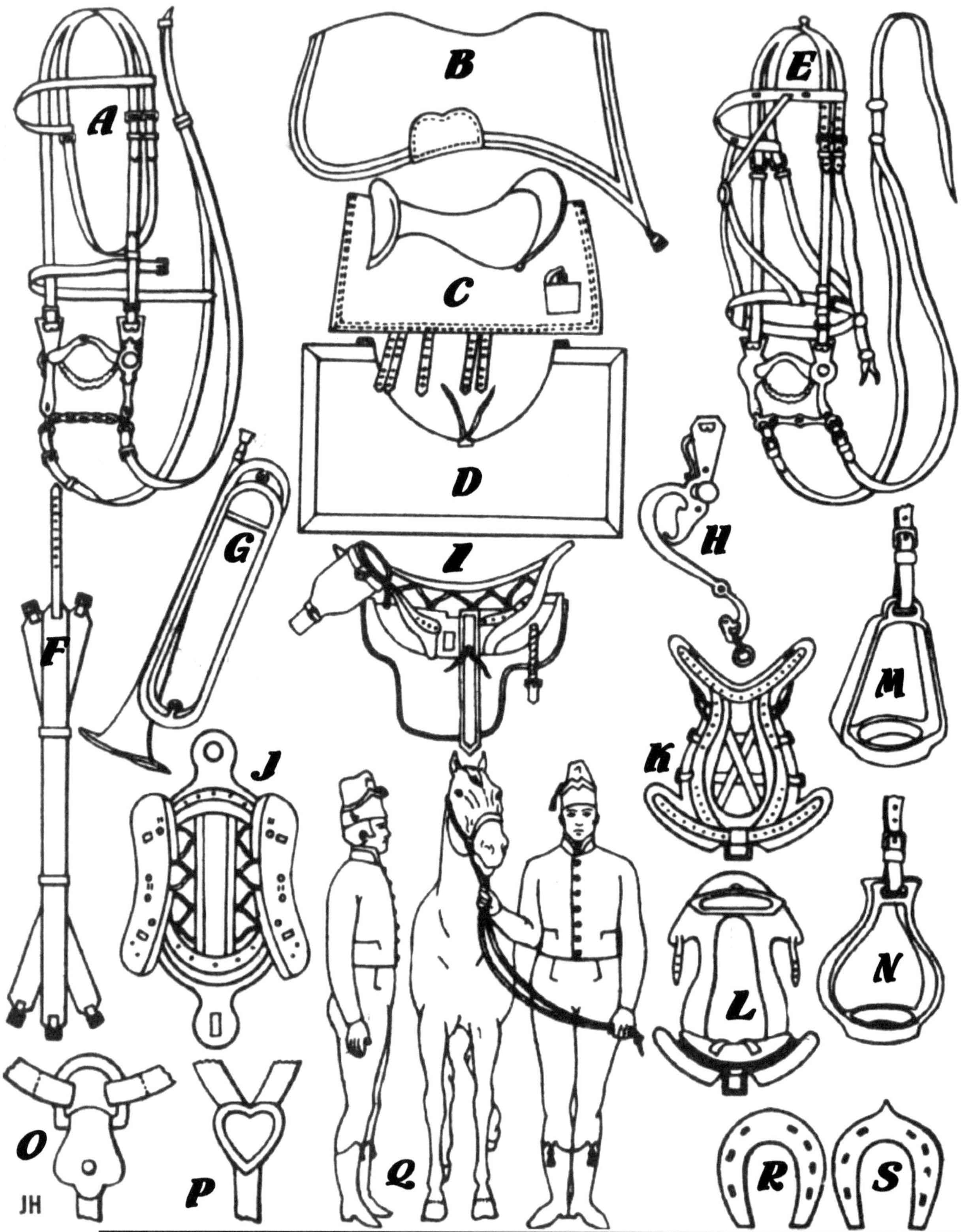

Cavalry, 1824: **A.** Headstall Line **B.** Light Shabrak **C.** Saddle w/Skirts **D.** Saddlecloth **E.** Light Headstall **F.** Cinch **G.** Trumpet **H.** Bit **I.** Saddle Tree **J.** Light Saddle Tree (top) **K.** Line Saddle Tree (bottom) **L.** Same (top) **M.** Line Stirrup **N.** Light Stirrup **O.** Line Breast Strap **P.** Light Breast Strap **Q.** Drill Uniforms **R.** Horseshoe, Right Foreleg **S.** Horse Shoe, Hind Leg

Plate II

A. Light Cavalry, 1835
B. Lt. Col. As Sgt. Major, Commandant of a Fortified Place, Gala Dress, 1835
C. Subaltern, Commandancy of a Fortified Place, Service Dress, 1835
D. Light Troop in Frock Coat, Rifle at "Rest Arms," 1835
E. Infantry, Back View

Plate III

Plate IV

A. 2nd Sergeant, 1st Regular Cavalry Regiment, 1839
B. Captain, 6th Regular Cavalry Regiment, 1839
C. Corporal, Light Regiment of Mexico, 1835
D. Lancer, 8th Regular Cavalry Regiment, 1839
E. Trooper, 7th Regular Cavalry Regiment, 1839

Plate V

A. Rifleman, 6th Regular Infantry Regiment w/Baker Rifle, 1839
B. Sub-Lieutenant Grenadier Company, 7th Regular Infantry Regiment, Sword Signal *Diana* ("Reveille"), 1839
C. Fifer, 11th Regular Infantry Regiment, Summer Field Dress, Barracks Cap, 1839
D. Drummer, 9th Regular Infantry Regiment, Drum & Baldric, 1839
E. Private, 8th Infantry, Active Militia, Tropical Region, 1839

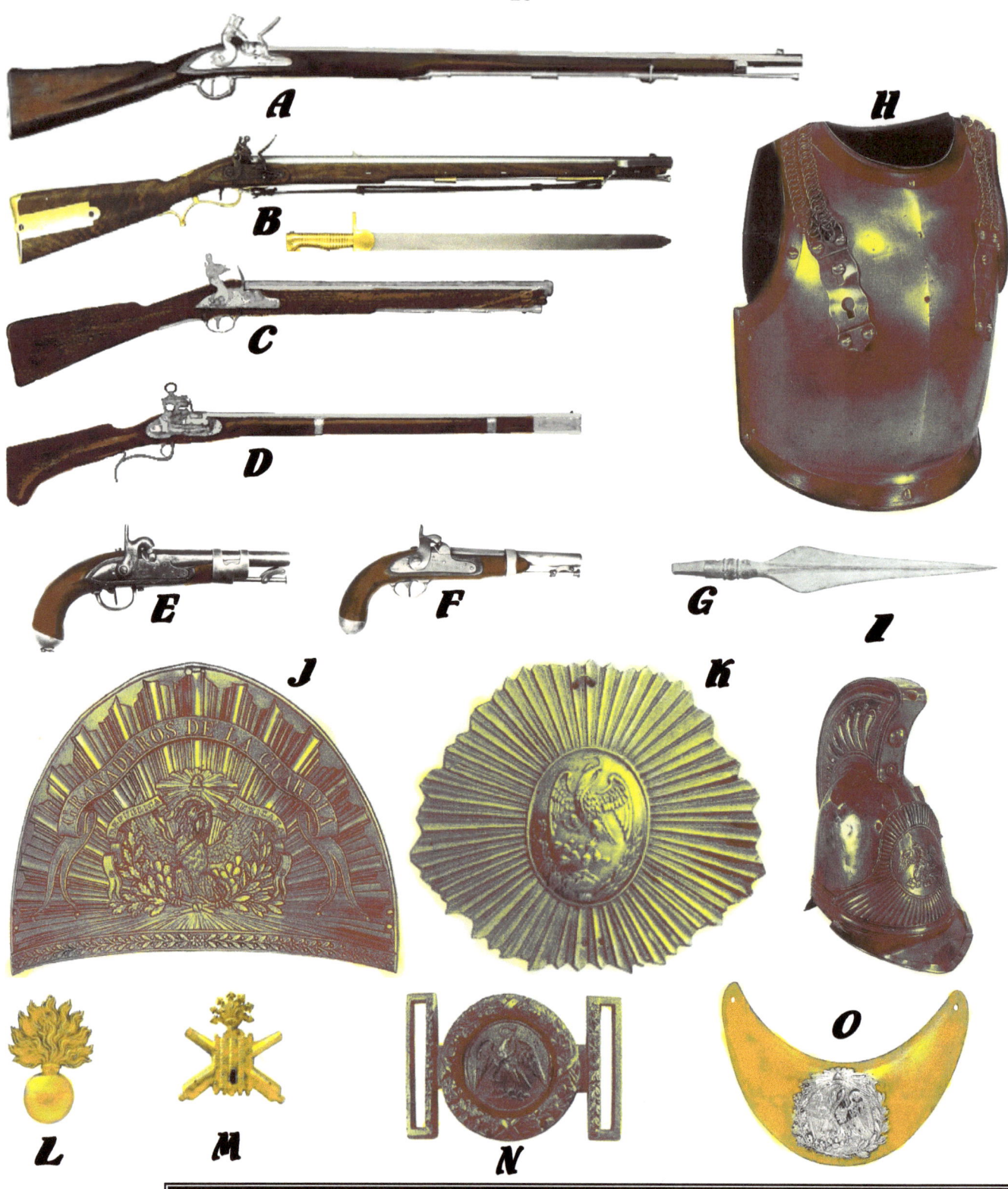

A. East India Pattern Musket **B.** Baker Rifle and Bayonet **C.** Tower Flintlock Carbine **D.** *Escopeta*—Shotgun/Blunderbuss type weapon commonly carried by Irregular Cavalry **E, F** Typical Cavalry Pistols (both converted to Percussion) **G.** Lance point as carried by Lancers and Territorial Cavalry **H.** Cuirass as worn by troopers of the Tulancingo Cuirassiers (chest ornament missing) **I.** Cuirassier's helmet (plume and chin chain missing) **J.** Bearskin plate (possibly for an Officer) of the Grenadiers of the Supreme Powers **K.** Smaller "generic" cap plate **L & M.** Cap Badges **N.** Officers Belt Buckle **O.** Officer's Gorget

Plate VI

Plate VII

A. California Presidial Co. Campaign Dress, 1839
B. California Presidial Co., Garrison Dress, 1839
C. Presidial Company, Dismounted, 1839
D. Four Time Deserter, 1839
E. Battalion of Invalids of Mexico, 1839

Plate VIII

A. Brigadier General, Half-Uniform, w/Cape, 1840
B. Division General, Gala Uniform, 1840
C. Corporal, Regular Light Infantry, 1840
D. Private, 3rd Line Infantry Regiment, 1840
E. Private, Regular Light Infantry, Field Dress with Cap, 1840
F. Private, National Guard in Frock Coat, 1840

Plate IX

A. Trooper, 6th Line Cavalry Regiment, 1840
B. Private, 4th Artillery Brigade, 1840
C. Captain, Mounted Artillery, Militia 1840
D. Officer of Engineers, 1840
E. Workman, Artillery Arsenal, 1840.

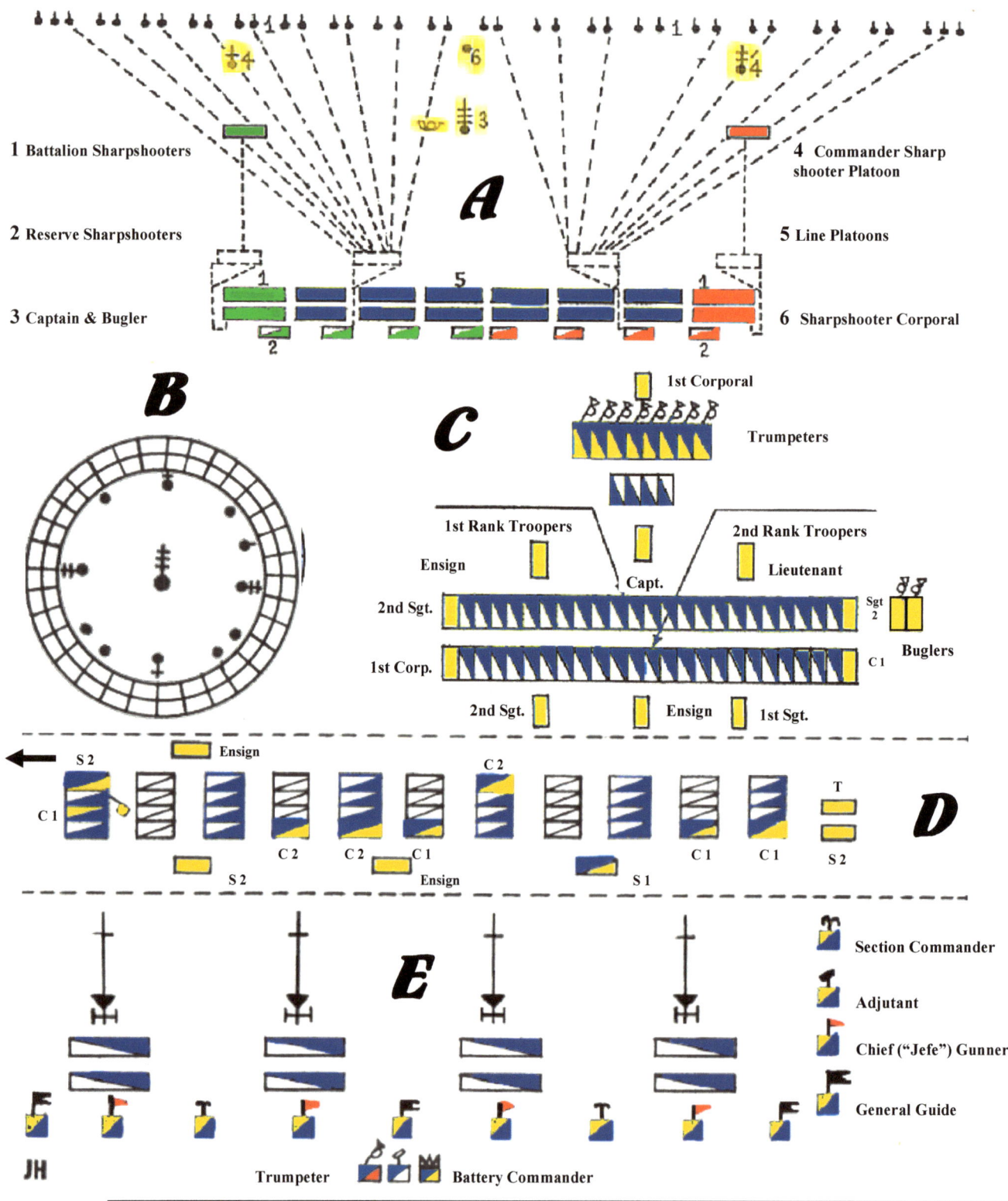

Plate X

Formations:
A. Light Infantry Battalion Sharpshooters Deploying
B. Circle Formation
C. Cavalry Squadron in Line
D. Cavalry Squadron in Column
E. Light Battery Deployed

Sword Signals: A. Orders B. Roll Call C. Assembly D. Halt E. March in Step F. Tattoo, Quick Step G. Prayer H. Grenadier March

Bayonet Drill: I. Free Thrust J. Thrust in Third K. Arms on High L. On Guard M. Parry in Prime N. Guard Position O. Circle by Fours

Plate XI

Plate XII

A. Grenadier, of the Grenadier Guards of the Supreme Powers, 1841
B. 1st Sergeant, Grenadiers, of the Grenadier Guards of the Supreme Powers, 1842
C. Trooper, 9th Regular Cavalry Regiment, New Uniform, 1841
D. Private, 11th Regular Infantry Regiment, New Uniform, 1842
E. Private, Marine Regiment, New Uniform, 1842

A. Lt. Colonel, General Staff, 1842
B. Corporal, Hussars, Guard of the Supreme Powers, 1843
C. Captain, Tulancingo Cuirassiers, Full Dress, 1842
D. 1st Sergeant, 7th Regular Cavalry Regiment, New Uniform, 1842
E. Jalisco Lancer, 1843

Plate XIII

Plate XIV

A. Southern Volunteer Cavalry, 1847
B. Line Cavalry w/Cape, 1843
C. Trooper, Mounted Rifles, 1843
D. Engineer's Tailcoat, Back View, 1847
E. Cowman's Saddle, Territorial Cavalry

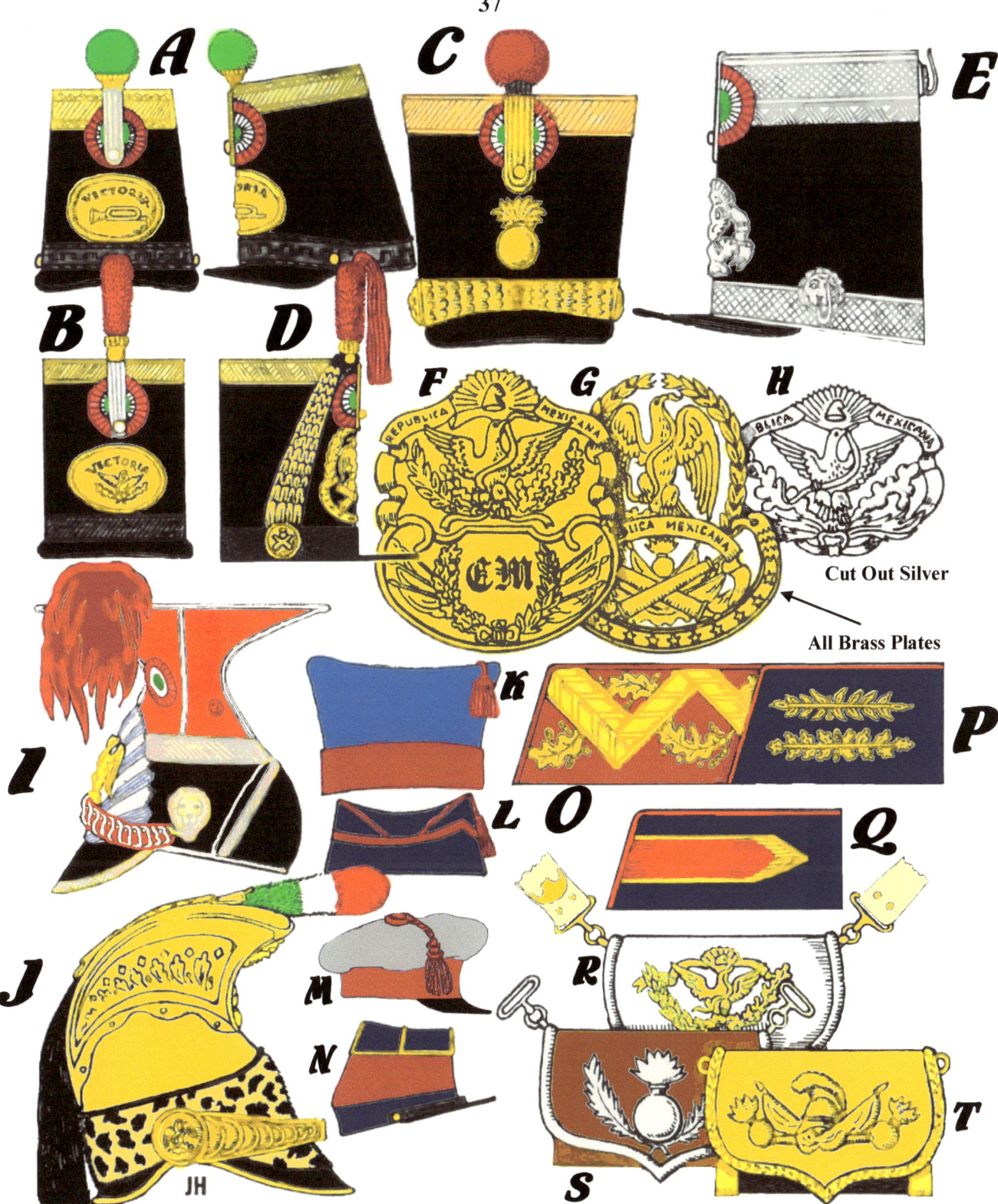

Headgear: A. National Guard, "Victoria" Battalion, Rifleman (two views) **B.** National Guard, possibly for a Grenadier **C.** Probable Line Grenadier Officer **D.** Artillery Officer **E.** Cavalry Staff Officer **Shako Shields: F.** Infantry **G.** Artillery **H.** Cavalry **Helmets: I.** Lancer Officer, 1840 **J.** Cuirassier Helmet **K-N.** Barracks/Garrison Caps **Collar Insignia: O.** Commissioner **P.** Hospital Professor, 1846 **Q.** 2nd Adjutant, Medical Corps, 1846 **Cartouches: R.** Cavalry **S.** Infantry **T.** Horse Artillery

Plate XV

Plate XVI

A. Private, 4th Light Infantry Battalion, 1846
B. Field Chaplain
C. Hospital Director, Medical Corps, Gala Dress, 1846
D. 1st Adjutant, Medical Corps, Field Dress, 1846
E. Ambulance Attendant, Field Dress, 1846
F. *Soldadera* ("Soldier Woman")
G. Trooper, 1st Regular Cavalry Regiment, New Uniform, 1845

Plate XVII — San Blas Battalion, First Review in Tepic, February 10, 1825

Plate XVIII — San Blas Battalion's "Last Stand" at Chapultepec, September 13, 1847

Mexican Military Academy, 1846-1847
A. Cadet, Service Uniform B. Engineer Officer/Instructor
C. Cadet Sub-lieutenant, Dress Uniform D. Cadet, Fatigue Uniform
E. Bandsman

Plate XIX

The Matamoros and Guerrero *Permanente* Battalions both fought in the Texas Campaign of 1836 and were at the Alamo. Both Colors shown were captured by forces under Texian General Sam Houston at San Jacinto on April 21, 1836.

1st *Activo* Battalion of Guanajuato. Though this unit also participated in the Texas Campaign, this surviving flag seems to date closer to the Mexican War.
Dimensions: 100 x 105 cm.

The Battalion of Invalids of Mexico. This unusual unit was part of the *Permanente* establishment for many years. This particular design is based on a later version and is partly conjectural as a representation for this period.

Plate XX — Flags

Mexican Flags tended to follow a fairly standard pattern: A tricolor of Green-White-Red, with Green alongside the staff and Red on the fly end. The eagle was always central (sometimes with either snake or cactus, not always both, and at least once with neither) though in many variants. Most flag devices and text were painted on, though some embroidery is in evidence.

Battalions/Regiments of the *Permanente* establishment apparently always had a bow, streamers, and/or cockade at the head of the staff. *Activo Milicia* and *Guardia Nacional* units had these only occasionally.

Flagstaffs could have spearheads or gold eagles inspired by Napoleonic designs.

The flags depicted are *not* to scale.

Example of Mexican National Colors, c. 1846.
Many display only the eagle and snake.
Dimensions: 639 x 459 cm.

First Activo Battalion of Morelia,
c. 1846
Dimensions: 62 x 102 cm.

Grenadiers of the Supreme Powers,
Also known as the Grenadiers of the
Guard. This design is partly
conjectural.

Coast Guard Battalion of Tampico.
Raised in 1823, participated in the
defense of Vera Cruz in March, 1847.
Dimensions: 116 x 123 cm.

Active Militia Battalion of
San Luis Potosí, c. 1847.
Dimensions: 113 x 102 cm.

Plate XXI

National Guard Free Battalion of Puebla,
raised in May, 1846, this unit saw action at
Vera Cruz in March, 1847.
Dimensions: 132 x 86 cm.

Guidon of the Fourth *Permanente* Light Infantry Regiment, c. 1847. Similar Guidons often have yellow and green colors reversed.
Dimensions: 72 x 74 cm.

Guidon of the 2nd Company (Fusiliers) of the 7th *Permanente* Regiment, c. 1847. The Light Company's Guidon is green with white lettering. Some patterns include an eagle in the center.
Dimensions: 50 x 50 cm.

Guidon of the Grenadier Company of the 12th *Permanente* Regiment, c. 1847.
Dimensions: 76 x 69 cm.

Lance Pennant carried by Guerrilla Cavalry unit in Central Mexico, 1847. Motto reads *No Doi Cuartel* ("I Give No Quarter")
Dimensions: 29 x 53 x 25 cm.

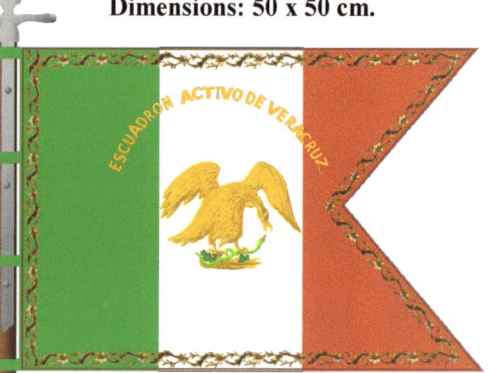

Standard of the *Activo Milicia* Squadron of Vera Cruz, captured upon the fall of the Port in 1847.
Dimensions: 60 x 84 x 50 cm.

Cavalry Guidon, one of several like it captured by US forces, c 1846.
Dimensions: 122 x 86 x 42cm.

Permanente Cavalry Regiment of Quatla, c. 1836
Dimensions: 71 x 87 x 57 cm.

Infantry Guidon (6th Regiment?). c. 1847.
Dimensions: 62 x 92 x 51 cm.

Plate XXII

Cavalry Standard of unidentified unit, captured at Cerro Gordo, reproduced to demonstrate its unusual tricolor design.
Dimensions: 76 x 133 x 54 cm.

ARMY REORGANIZATION OF DECEMBER, 1835

New Infantry Battalion Identities	Created From Previous Battalions Numbered:	New Cavalry Regiment Identities	Created From Previous Regiments Numbered:
Hidalgo	1st & 2nd	Dolores	3rd & 6th
Allende	3rd	Iguala	4th & 10th
Morelos	4th	Palmar	2nd, 7th, & Active Regiment of Mexico
Guerrero	5th	Cuautla	11th & 12th
Aldama	6th	Vera Cruz	5th & 9th
Jimenez	7th & 12th	Tampico	1st & 8th
Landero	8th & 9th	Yucatan Squadron	No Change
Abasolo	11th	Tampico Company	
Matamoros	10th	Battalion names being of distinguished leaders in the War of Independence	
Galeana	13th		
The 8 Standing Companies became the Acapulco, San Blas, Tampico, 1st & 2nd Bacalar, Carmen Island, and 1st & 2nd Tabasco		Regimental names all being those of battlefields associated with the Independence Movement.	

    Regular Cavalry transformed into Light Troops followed the law of Sept. 1st 1824 for their organization and drew Lancers' pay. They were dressed like the Light Infantry but with helmet instead of shako and white metal buttons; their training, drill and equipment following the Spanish Cavalry tactics reprinted in Mexico by Galvan in 1824 (PL. III-a).

    According to these, the standard Line Cavalry and Dragoon saddle had a wood frame with iron plates covered with leather and stuffed with horsehair in canvas cushions, iron stirrups and leather pistol holsters. The carbine rested in a cylindrical leather boot at the right side of the saddle, muzzle and ramrod facing down. Dragoons had a leather quiver in which to insert the rifle butt and a sling nailed to the saddle front to hold the firearm in place. Hussar and Mounted Rifle (Light Cavalry) saddles had a pointed knob with hole to attach shabraque, pelt or cloak (PL. II-j).

Active Commerce Regiment of Mexico

    This unit was raised April 12th 1835 only to be extinguished together with the 5th line Regiment for rebellion on July 20, 1839. Its original uniform as of June 5th, 1835, was quite flashy with a turkish blue tailcoat and 8 yellow lace trimmed buttonholes instead of lapels, the collar, cuffs and bars of black velvet with red arabesques and red piping; pants were dark blue or white.

1836

    In 1836, the Commerce Battalion of Mexico, followed by other regular and reserve Infantry units, abused the wearing of vertical flashes on cuffs, a distinction reserved for preference Companies only. An order had to be circulated to restrict the use of a single flash to Grenadier and Rifle Companies, and the double flash to preference Companies formed within columns consisting entirely of Grenadiers or of Riflemen (PL. V-a, b).

    To prevent waste and administer efficiently the sizable sums provided by the national treasury for the subsistence of the army on the move to Texas "…Being drawn from a sacred fund in the anguished circumstances in which the public finances existed…" it was decreed in October 1836 that all accounting operations be performed by a special section of competent functionaries charged specifically with the han-

Mexican Light Cavalry Trooper
Ready for Santa Anna's Texas Campaign of 1836. Dress: dark blue coat, gray trousers, red piping and white metal. Veterans of Regular Cavalry were selected for this service and received higher pay. Their organization and tactics were based on Spanish Regulations of 1824.
(Illustration courtesy of the Old Army Press)

dling of sums consigned to the army in Texas. A Division Commissioner, an Accountant, a Treasurer, two First, Second and Third Officers and 6 clerks were stationed at a central point to make resources available punctually to the army and to its detached divisions. A Provider of Food and Supplies, a Storekeeper and a Paymaster with 2 clerks were added. The Commissioner was subject to a bond of 10,000 *pesos* and received the pay of his rank with a bonus of 3,000 *pesos* a year; the Accountant and Treasurer deposited a 4,000 *peso* bond and enjoyed a bonus of 2,000; the Officers received bonuses of 1,000, 800 and 600 respectively while the clerks drew straight pay of 800 *pesos* from the day of departure to the day of return.

The General HQ Staff of the Army of the North for the campaign against Texas was quite numerous. There was the General in Chief and the QM General who combined his duties with those of a Major General of Infantry, Cavalry and Dragoons and of the Inspector of these three branches. A First Adjutant General was in charge of encampments, another one of discipline and supplies plus the functions of an Infantry and Cavalry General Major, another General Adjutant in charge of train, one Captain Adjutant with a troop of 30 Guides for terrain reconnaissance, 18 officers as adjutants and clerks, and Army Justice Department with a Commissioner-Intendent, an Accountant, Treasurer with Personnel, a Military Health Corps Inspector, Hospital Directors, 4 unattached Surgeons and 8 Practicants.

Marching with the army was also a Military Vicar General with Chaplains for every corps, an Assessor General as Army Field Auditor and finally a Police Captain with a detachment of 25 to 30 cavalrymen with their Sergeants and Corporals, all chosen for good conduct and courage to keep watch over law and order in encampments and on marches.

Artillery, Engineers and Sappers had their own Sub-inspectors and Directors. In the line of battle, Engineer officers and the QM stood at the side of the General in Chief to help lead columns, establish strong points, reconnoiter rivers, fords and bridges, repair or open up roads and direct attack or defense on harbors and garrisons.

1837

With the advent of 1837, fifteen months after the opening of major hostilities with Texas, the Mexican Army reached a reasonably well organized state.

On April 11th, after some suggestions to abolish firearms in the Cavalry altogether, it was decreed that "… The 1st Company of all Cavalry Regiments shall be of Lancers, made up of individuals with the aptitude and other requisites to perform this service…."

Independent Companies and Squadrons were to have a squad of 8 Lancers and a Corporal each, with a Second Sergeant and an Ensign in command of all the Lancer squads.

1838

On April 16, a French fleet blockaded Mexican harbors and coasts.

On Nov. 27, 4 French frigates, 2 corvettes, 2 gunboats and 2 brigantines with a total of 150 cannon and mortars opened a bombardment and forced Ulua Castle to capitulate. Three days later, Nov. 30, the government called in Santa Anna to head the Mexican Army and to make war against Louis Philippe of

France. Santa Anna reported resplendent in a blue tailcoat with red plastron richly gold embroidered with laurel leaves, cream colored pants and the tail feathers of fighting cocks waving from his hat. In the street battle with a landing force of French sailors and naval gunners, Santa Anna lost his left leg, but gained the coveted appellation of having "…Deserved well of the fatherland…" as well as his first try at the interim presidency of the republic.

On June 30 the army was increased to 60,000 men "…To defend the nation against any foreign aggression and to conserve order within…" but shortage of officers and men caused that an Infantry Company with only 34 men could have just one Lieutenant in command; if it fell below that strength, its officer was retired and the rank-and-file distributed among other Companies. A Company of 50 men would have a Captain and Lieutenant, of 68 men a Captain, Lieutenant, and Sub-lieutenant.

A Cavalry unit of 23 men had a Lieutenant only, 34 men rated a Captain, and a Lieutenant, 46 men an additional Ensign and only a 68 man Company was entitled to a complete officers' staff.

Sept. 14 the Artillery Corps was reorganized as a regular Field and Garrison force with 3 foot and 1 mounted Brigades bearing Flags and Guidons, 5 standing Companies, the HQ staff, a paymaster section and a Company of arsenal workers. A Brigade had 8 Companies, each with 66 artillerists, 20 noncoms, 2 buglers and drummers and 3 officers in peace time, and 5 officers, 22 noncoms, 86 gunners and 2 buglers and drummers on war footing.

A foot Brigade HQ staff had 5 senior and 6 junior officers, a Captain Paymaster, a Chaplain and a Surgeon, a First Brigade Sergeant, a Drum and Bugle Major, an Armorer, 8 Pioneers with a Corporal, 12 musicians and 2 bandmasters. A Mounted Brigade had 6 Companies, each with 66 gunners, 2 trumpeters, 20 noncoms, 4 officers, 88 saddle and 50 draft horses; its HQ staff was the same as in foot Brigades but with a Trumpet Major, a Groom Marshall, 2 Saddlers, an Armorer and 8 Pioneers with their Corporal.

General Corps HQ consisted of 25 senior officers with insignia of Squadron or Battalion commanders.

On the same date, the Engineer Corps was set up with a Brigadier General as Director, 10 senior and 40 junior officers, a Sapper Battalion of 600 men in 6 Companies, of which the 1st and 2nd of Miners and Pontoniers were equivalent to line Grenadiers with 3 buglers per Company; the other 4 Companies had 3 officers, 5 noncoms, 2 drummers and a fifer and 78 Sappers each.

1839

In February Army Headquarters Staff was enlarged and strengthened by a body of 32 captains and lieutenant attachés.

March 16, a general reorganization of all Infantry and Cavalry corps was undertaken. The army of the line (*Permanente*) was to consist of Infantry, Cavalry, Artillery and Engineers, grouped in 6 divisions of 2 to 4 Brigades, each Brigade with 2 to 4 Regiments, usually mixed foot and mounted units. An Infantry Regiment consisted of 2 Battalions with 8 Companies each, and a Cavalry or Dragoon Regiment of 4 squadrons with 2 Companies each. Three or more Divisions constituted an Army.

There were 12 regular Infantry Regiments, 8 Regular Cavalry and Dragoon Regiments—designated by consecu-

Mexican Regular Cavalry Lancer, 1839. Colors of tailcoat, trousers, and facing varied with each of the eight Regiments. Regimental number was stamped on buttons and embroidered on collar. A Regular (*Permanente*) Cavalry Regiment consisted of four Squadrons with two Companies each. Since 1837, the 1st Company of the 1st Squadron consisted of Lancers. Active Militia (*Activo Milicia*) Cavalry had only 8 Lancers per Company, with a Lance Corporal in charge; in action, they were converged into one Lancer unit led by an Ensign and a 2nd Sergeant.
(*Illustration courtesy of the Old Army Press*)

tive numbers respectively—and 1 special Squadron. The Artillery had 3 Brigades, 5 Foot Companies, a Mounted Brigade and a Sapper Battalion.

Infantry regimental HQ staff included a Colonel, Lieutenant Colonel, a Commandant, 2 Second Adjutants, 2 Lieutenants, 2 Ensign-Sub-lieutenants, 2 Surgeons, 2 Chaplains, a Drum Major and a Bugle Corporal, 2 Pioneer Corporals with 16 Pioneers and 2 armorers.

Six Fusilier, one Rifleman and one Grenadier Company formed the Battalion, each Company with 80 privates, a Captain, a Lieutenant, 2 Sub-lieutenants, one First and 4 Second Sergeants, 9 Corporals, a drummer, bugler and fifer in Fusilier and Grenadier Companies, and 4 buglers in the Rifle Company. Each Regiment had a Second Sergeant as tailor, and a Corporal blacksmith, mason and baker.

The 8 regimental Cavalry Companies contained each a Captain, a Lieutenant, 2 Ensigns, one First and 3 Second Sergeants, 9 Corporals, 2 trumpeters, 52 mounted and 8 dismounted troopers. Regimental HQ staff comprised the Colonel, a Lieutenant Colonel, 2 Squadron Commandants, 4 Adjutant Lieutenants, 4 Guidon Bearer Ensigns, a Chaplain, Surgeon, First Sergeant Marshall, 3 grooms, 1 Cornet Major and a Cornet Corporal, 2 Second Sergeants, saddler and armorer, 2 Corporals tailor and carpenter, and 3 troopers as shoemaker, mason and baker, all mounted.

The Active Militia (*Activo Milicia*) comprised 9 Infantry and 6 Cavalry Regiments with the same personnel as Regular Army units, and embodied a Veterinary School under a Cavalry lieutenant instructor. This personnel arrangement was typical and remained in force, with minor variations, until the end of the war in 1847.

Aug. 19, replacement centers were set up in Mexico and San Luis with 4 Infantry Companies and 1 Cavalry Squadron each; no special uniform was indicated for these center units.

By law of July 8, the regimental numbers of the forces reorganized March 16 were distributed by seniority and by location in the following manner:

Two days later, distinctive uniforms for these Regular Infantry and Cavalry Regiments were decreed; these were substituted on Aug. 31 1840, but restored again and confirmed Dec. 22 1841. The July 10, 1839 Infantry dress consisted of a tailcoat and long pants of turkish blue cloth with cloth facings in a combination of distinctive colors different for every unit.

\multicolumn{4}{c}{**INFANTRY REGIMENTAL REORGANIZATION OF MARCH 16, 1839**}
Number	1st Battalion	Formed From	2nd Battalion/Replacement Cadre
1	Morelos (P)	Activo of Guadalajara	Guanajuato
2	Hidalgo (P)	Tres Villas	Vera Cruz
3	Allende (P)	Activo of Querétaro	Jalisco
4	Guerrero (P)	Activo of San Luis Potosí	San Luis
5	Aldama (P)	Activo of Mexico	Mexico
6	Jimenez (P)	Public Security Force of Mexico	Mexico
7	Matamoros (P)	Activo of Puebla	Puebla
8	Landero (P)	Yucatán Auxiliary	Vera Cruz
9	Abasolo (P)	Activo of Chiapas	Oaxaca-Chiapas
10	Galeana (P)	Activo of Yucatán	Yucatán
11	Toluca (A)	Activo of Mextitlán	Mexico-Querétaro
12	Tlaxcala (A)	Activo of Mexico	Puebla-Tlaxcala
(P)= *Permanente* (Regular) (A)=*Activo Milicia* (Militia)			

CAVALRY REGIMENTAL REORGANIZATION OF MARCH 16, 1839

Number	Formed From	Replacement Cadre
1	(P) Tampico and Activo of San Luis Potosí	San Luis Potosí
2	(P) Vera Cruz and Activo of Zacatecas	Zacatecas
3	(P) Dolores and Activo Squadron of Durango	Durango
4	(P) Iguala and Auxiliaries of the Cold Country	Querétaro
5	(P) Palmar and 1st & 2nd Activo of Jalisco	Jalisco
6	(P) Cuautla and Activo Squadron of Morelia	Guanajuato
7	(P) Mexico and Cuernavaca Squadron, Auxiliaries of Ayotla, Chalco, Texcoco, & Tulancingo	Mexico
8	(A) of Puebla & Activo Squadron of Tlaxcala	Yucatán
Special Squadron	Yucatán	Yucatán
(P)= *Permanente* (Regular) (A)=*Activo Milicia* (Militia)		

Plain white canvas pants were worn in summer by all.

Some contemporary prints show Infantry using white gaiters over the shoes although none of the uniform regulations, contracts or inventories list such.

Cavalry dress was more colorful and varied than Infantry, consisting of a tailcoat and pants with

INFANTRY UNIFORM COLOR REGULATIONS OF JULY 10, 1839

Battalion #	Collar	Lapels/Vest	Cuffs	Bars	Piping
1	Yellow	Blue or White	Deep Red	Deep Red	Yellow
2	Sky Blue	Deep Red	Deep Red	Deep Red	Deep Red
3	Sky Blue	Crimson	Crimson	Crimson	Sky Blue
4	Sky Blue	Deep Red	Sky Blue	Deep Red	White
5	Deep Red	Deep Red	Sky Blue	Deep Red	Sky Blue
6	Crimson	White	Crimson	Crimson	*Opposite Colors
7	Green	Gold embroidered button holes instead of Lapels	Green	Crimson	Crimson
8	Deep Red	Sky Blue	Deep Red	Sky Blue	Opposite Colors
9	Buff	Purple	Purple	Buff	Opposite Colors
10	Deep Red	Purple	Purple	Deep Red	Buff
11†	Deep Red	Green	Deep Red	Deep Red	Opposite Colors
12	Buff	Buff	Buff	Deep Red	Opposite Colors

* "Opposite Colors" implies that the collar is piped with the color of the lapels, and the lapels with the color of the collar, etc. (PL. V-a, b, c, d, e)

† On 12/22/39, this Regiment was assigned a white tailcoat, with Sky Blue Collar, Lapels, and Cuffs, with Deep Red Cuff Bars, Piping in Opposite Colors, and Sky Blue Trousers with Red Seam Stripe. On 6/30/42 the Trousers were changed again to Crimson with White Seam Stripe

seat lining of antelope skin. Regimental colors were as follows.

Uniform accessories for Infantry were yellow (brass), for Cavalry white (silver), the regimental number stamped on all buttons and embroidered on collar. Any extra embroidery on collar or sleeves was prohibited except coattail clasps in the form of eagles 2" wide between wingtips.

Both Infantry and Cavalry used the shako, somewhat different in shapes but all with front plates

CAVALRY UNIFORM COLOR REGULATIONS OF JULY 10, 1839

Regiment #	Tail Coat	Trousers	Collar	Lapels/ Vest	Cuffs	Bars	Piping	Saddle Blanket/ Valise/Etc
1*	Yellow	Medium Blue	Deep Red	Deep Red	Deep Red	Deep Red	†Opposite Colors	Deep Red
2	Yellow	Turkish Blue	Sky Blue	Sky Blue	Sky Blue	Sky Blue	Sky Blue	Turkish Blue
3	Turkish Blue		Green	White	Green	—	Opposite Colors	Green
4	Sky Blue	Turkish Blue	Deep Red	Deep Red	Deep Red	Deep Red	Opposite Colors	Green
5	Turkish Blue		Deep Red	Deep Red	Deep Red	Deep Red	Opposite Colors	Deep Red
6	Green		White	White	White	Deep Red	None	Deep Red
7‡	White	Turkish Blue	Sky Blue	Sky Blue	Sky Blue	Sky Blue	None	Green
8	Turkish Blue		White	Deep Red	Deep Red	White	None	Green
9#	Green	Dark Blue w/Crimson Seam Stripe	Crimson	Crimson	Crimson	Crimson	White	Green

* On 9/7/45 this Regiment was assigned a Dark Green Tailcoat, Gray Trousers with Red Seam Stripe, Dark Green Collar & Cuffs, Yellow Lapels and Bars with Yellow Piping and a Deep Red Saddle Blanket with Green Valise with White straps.
† "Opposite Colors" implies that the collar is piped with the color of the lapels, and the lapels with the color of the collar, etc. (PL. IV-a, b, d, e, PL. XII, c)
‡ 9/10/39, this Regiment was assigned a Crimson Tailcoat with Green Collar, Lapels, Cuffs and Bars, 8 White lace trimmed buttonholes, piping in opposite colors, Green Pants with Crimson Seam Stripe and Sky Blue Saddle Blanket with a White band (PL. XIII-d).
# Raised in late 1841, and assigned this uniform on 6/30/42.

Azul Turqui

A comment is necessary on the prevalent uniform color specified as "turkish blue" that met with a variety of interpretations by government agencies and contractors, fluctuating from a blue-black through varying shades of dark and medium blue. Etymologically, turkish blue is the band of darkest blue in the spectrum, but in colloquial use in Spanish-speaking regions it frequently designates medium or turquoise blue; the word "blue" (*azul*) alone means a cobalt blue, while expressions such as dark blue, blue-black, military blue, etc, refer specifically to deep blue shades.

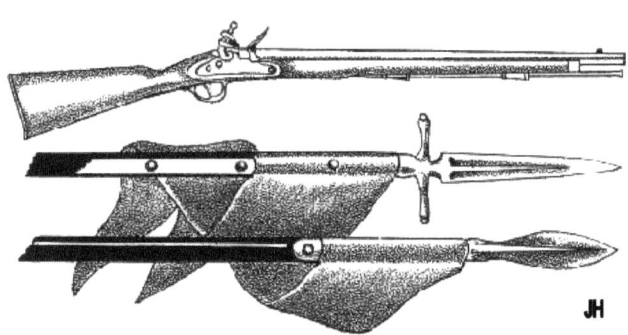

(Top) Mexican Cavalry Carbine, British surplus model of 1801, carried suspended from a hook on a carbine belt.
(Middle) Standard 1824 regulation Cavalry Lance, Spanish model (full description, page 15).
(Bottom) Lance of Militia and Irregular units, converted from pikes used to herd cattle on the range. Usually a crude, home-made product.
(Illustration courtesy of the Old Army Press)

bearing the national coat or arms and unit number (PL— XV).*

January 26 a mounted Light Commerce Regiment of Mexico was established with 4 squadrons of 2 Companies each, the 1st Squadron including a Corporal's squad of Pioneers drawing Dragoon's pay.

The Light Mounted Regiment of Mexico

Originally raised in 1835, this unit dressed in a sky blue coatee, with scarlet red collar, cuffs, bars and epaulettes, dark blue Cavalry pants with deep red stripes at seams and leather half-boots, the regular Cavalry model ornamented shako, a sky blue cloak, saddle blanket, holster covers and saddle roll all edged with scarlet cloth bands (PL. IV-c). The same dress was also used by a Light Regiment of Vera Cruz, the Yucatan Squadron, the Puebla Light Squadron, a regular Tabasco Company and all Active Militia Cavalry except the Mounted Rifles and the Jalisco Lancers.

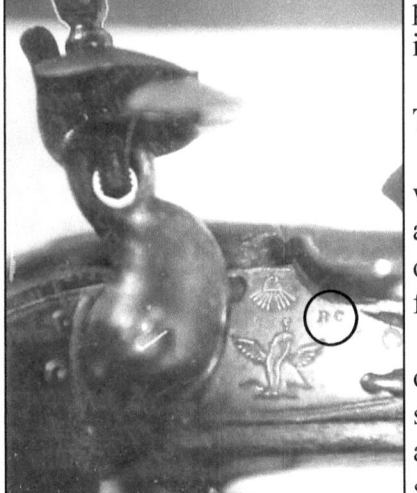

Lock plate and Mexican Government markings on an army musket used during the Texas and Mexican-American Wars. The regimental stamp "RC" (circled) stands for *Regimento de Commercio* that made its last stand at the defense of the Churubusco Convent. Original weapon in the possession of R. H. Bettels, USA.
(Illustration courtesy of the Old Army Press)

The Active Commerce Regiment of Mexico

Formed on March 16, 1839, as a privileged unit, the officers' corps was restricted to wealthy merchants or professional men of good conduct, age and education, and the sons of owners of productive businesses; an officer who went bankrupt in his civilian business was not eligible for further promotion.

Retirement was conditioned by pecuniary services for the benefit of the Regiment. All served without pay, at their own expense, compensated—as they said—by the honor of a decorous service for themselves and useful to the fatherland. Sergeants had to prove good conduct, disposition and education, preference being given to men of property, capital, business or a decent trade.

The Regiment maintained a common fund for their uniforms and arms replacements, the manufacture of uniforms being determined by a council of Captains and Commandants. Flags, arms, drums, and Infantry sabers for Grenadiers and riflemen were furnished free from any army warehouses. The Regiment's duties were limited to the city area except in case of enemy invasion, and its principal task was to maintain order and security for property and persons in the capital. The unit had the standard 2 Battalions of 8 Companies and its HQ staff was nicknamed "Polka Dancers" (*polkos*) by the people.†

In addition to the regular units listed above, a variety of reserve and regional bodies performed field and garrison services, each with some peculiar distinction in dress. Many cities and departments raised their own independent Regiments or squadrons that frequently adopted the uniforms of some of the Regular Army units nearest to their state.

*A more detailed description of shakos is given on page 21.
†There seem to be two theories as to this nickname's origin: 1) This Officer Corps simply reveled in the dance, and 2) Their uniforms were so gaudy they looked less like Soldiers and more like performers!

The New Uniform Regulations of 1840

On August 31, 1840, barely one year after the July 10, 1839 law, new regulations were issued introducing different uniforms and insignia for generals, officers and troops of the Army of the Republic. It was the first carefully edited and detailed dress regulation for all ranks and branches since Mexico had achieved its political independence, and furnishes a vivid description of the outward appearance of officers and men even though the original model drawings no longer exist.

Common provisions for all 1840 uniforms were: With their half-uniform, Sub-lieutenants and Ensigns wore shoulder loops of 5-stranded lace on their left side, Lieutenants on right side, Captains on both. Former First Adjutants, not Battalion or Squadron Commandants, had two shoulder loops of 8-strand lace embroidered in a mixture of gold and silver. Lieutenant Colonels and Colonels displayed the 1839 insignia.

Half-uniform was understood as plain turkish blue tailcoat and pants with collar, cuffs, bars and piping of the same color, and gold or silver accessories for Infantry and Cavalry respectively. Infantry, Cavalry, Artillery and Engineers wore a turkish blue round jacket for daily service in garrison, at drill and on marches. White jackets and pants were prohibited except in excessively hot regions.

The uniform specified in the above law was to be standard, without any differentiation between Infantry, Cavalry, Artillery Brigades and standing Companies except for their unit numbers on collars and shakos.

Officers' Dress

Generals' gala uniform consisted of a turkish blue tailcoat with bright red piping, lapels, cuffs, bars and collar, and a ½" wide gold embroidered design of interlaced palm, laurel and olive branches around collar, cuffs and lapels, two rows of this embroidery on Division General's cuffs and one row on Brigadier General's, horizontal pockets with gold embroidered flaps and 3 eagle buttons, and coattails clasps in the form of large eagles 4" wide across wingspread. Epaulets were of heavy gold with 3" bullion fringes, the strap in raised leaf-work and a white eagle in the center of each blade. A sky blue sash with 5" gold fringes and knots with 2 rows of embroidery signified a Division General, and a green one with the same fringes but one row of embroidery on knots a Brigadier General.

Trousers were turkish blue with 1" wide gold stripes at seams. A black fore-and-aft bicorn described as three-point hat, displaying a 2" wide undulated lace, was garnished with a white plume around the edges, had loop and tassels of gold bullion and was topped with three 9" long plumes in the national colors in addition to a 3" diameter tricolor cockade under the gold loop; it seems however, that a loose tuft of rooster feathers in the 3 colors was used more frequently.

A straight sword in a black frog was suspended under the tailcoat, a metallic gold tassel tied to the guard. A cane with black silk tassels and chamois colored gloves completed the gala dress. Overcoat or cape are not specified.

The service half-uniform consisted of a turkish blue tailcoat with cuffs of same color and no piping, but with the regulation embroidery on collar and cuffs, same buttons and clasps but without pocket flaps, with or without epaulettes, plain turkish blue pants without stripes or piping, the gala sash, and the hat without tricolor plumes.

Generals could also appear in civilian type clothes combined with their sash with gold embroidered insignia under tailcoat or frock coat. All embroidery and trimmings of the gala uniform and saddle were of gold.

The saddle was mixed ranch-type and military model, all leather parts black with gilt ornaments, but precious stones set in the saddles were prohibited. The gala saddle blanket and triple holster covers were of scarlet cloth edged with 2 rows of gold lace, the outer one 2-1/2", the inner one 1" wide; a gold embroidered rising eagle of 5" wingspread appeared in the hind corner of the blanket. With half and campaign uniforms, the saddle blanket and holster covers were turkish blue with a single 2" wide gold lace edging.

For mounted wear with either uniform, turkish blue pants without stripe and high boots with white boot-hose, spurs with straight bar and strap were prescribed. The gold lace stripe on pants, gold sword knot and gilt eagle button were specifically generals' insignia and no other rank was permitted to use them (PL. VIII-a, b).

Infantry officers from Colonel down used the 1839 type of epaulettes, but glittering fringes, collar and cuff embroidery, larger clasps, lace or cords on pants, plaited lace and piping or any other unauthorized ornaments were prohibited. Infantry sword knots were deep red without metallic strands. Senior officers carried canes with silk cords, but junior officers temporarily in senior posts were not entitled to canes.

When mounted, officers used a mixed model black saddle and reins with brass buckles. Saddle blankets and holster covers were of turkish blue cloth with 2" wide deep red cloth stripes around. All officers carried sword-sabers on waist belts under the tailcoat in the field, and suspended from a cross belt with frog in garrison, and wore shakos and plain white cotton gloves.

Bicorn hats were prohibited for all except General Staff officers and Quartermaster Office personnel.

Cavalry Officers wore the same uniform as troopers but of finer cloth, with cartouche box, cross belt and waist belt of white leather (some cartouche boxes still existing are of brown leather), brass buckles, plates and bars, and green sword knots. Both curved sabers and straight swords were used according to the nature of the service (PL. IX-a).

Artillery Officers wore the uniform of their respective Brigade or Company of finer cloth, their lapels of black velvet, and gold lace or embroidery instead of yellow silk.
Saddle blankets and holster covers were the same as for troops but of better material. When dismounted, officers carried a straight sword on waist belt, when mounted, a saber on black slings, with yellow metal furnishings and a crimson silk sword knot at the grip.

Arsenal and Factory workers wore Foot Artillery items with a short jacket instead of tailcoat, and instead of the shako a round hat with narrow brim and corps emblem (PL IX-e). Arsenal officers used the uniform of Foot Artillery officers.

Artillery accounting employees wore a turkish blue tailcoat cut straight with wide coattails, gilt buttons with bomb, gold embroidered bombs on collar, the collar and cuffs edged with indented tape for First, Second and Third Officer; Commissioners used an embroidery pattern decreed Dec. 4, 1822, (PL XV -o) with current insignia of rank, turkish blue pants, bicorn hat without lace or plume and straight sword on black belt.

Artillery Justice Officers' dress was similar to Engineers but the tailcoat was straight cut with wide coattails, Assessors and Prosecutors distinguished by a serrated gold embroidery around edge of collar and cuffs, bomb on collar and a silver castle superimposed on it, with gilt buttons, turkish blue pants, bicorn hat without lace or plume, and straight sword on black belt.

Civilian clothes were prohibited to all officers from Colonel down. Regulation uniform and accessories were obligatory for all officers and troops when in formation, on and off duty and on marches. Outside of formation, they could wear a military frock coat with corresponding insignia; off duty and inside quarters officers could wear barracks caps of their respective branches of service. In and out of formation, whenever troops wore frock or overcoats, officers could wear them too, displaying their insignia.

The use of earrings, rings and other types of feminine ornaments that "Lower the military profession" were prohibited, offenders being subject to 1 month in prison for a first offense, 2 months for a second and 4 months of fortress for a third transgression.

Infantry Dress

The line Infantry dress was standardized for all units as a turkish blue tailcoat with scarlet collar, cuffs, bars and piping and plain yellow buttons, regimental numbers 2" high gold embroidered on collar without any other ornament; 3-pointed vertical pocket flaps with a button at each point in rear skirts; coat-tail clasps took the shape of a pair of 2" long quivers jointed at their bottom points, with 3 arrows in each. Pants were sky blue with deep red piping at seams. The black leather shako was conical with bank at crown, cockade loop and chinstrap of yellow metal and a 3" diameter tricolor cockade above a shield with national coat of arms and regimental number. None of the shakos still existing show a top metal band or metal cockade loop; the bands are of yellow, reddish or black lace, the loops of light or dark cord, both with metallic threads intertwined; there are however examples of shakos with the bottom cinch band of a brass or copper type metal.

All accessories for Infantry were yellow; pompon and shoulder straps were crimson for Pioneers, Grenadiers, Riflemen and Fusiliers alike (PL. VIII-c).

Light Infantry units wore a turkish blue tailcoat with deep red piping, spherical yellow buttons and the initial "L" (*Ligero*) embroidered in simplest form on the right, and "P" (*Permanente*) on the left side of the collar signifying "Light Permanent." For daily and field service, a grey jacket with red piping was worn instead of the tailcoat. Pants and overcoats were a grey mixture of black and white with deep red piping. The shako was smaller than for line Infantry, with top bank at crown, chinstrap and loop for tricolor cockade all of black patent leather, a green pompon and a brass bugle as emblem in front; the cross belts were of dull black leather without shield, held up by shoulder straps of the same color as the coat, with deep red piping around (PL. VIII-c, e).

No distinction is mentioned to tell apart the three Light Regiments.*

Cavalry Dress

Line Cavalry wore standard sky blue coatees with scarlet collars, cuffs, bars, piping and epaulettes, plain white metal buttons, 3-pointed buttoned vertical pocket flaps in back of skirts, coattail clasps in same form as Infantry and 2" high regimental numbers on collar. Pants were turkish blue with antelope skin seat lining, a leather half-boot, a two-finger wide trim and a 1" wide deep red stripe at side seams. The shako was the same as for Infantry but with white accessories. Cape, saddle blanket and roll, and holster covers were sky blue with 2" wide scarlet stripes all around except the saddle roll with a ½" stripe around the sides and on cover. Buckskin gloves with white gauntlets, a mixed saddle with yellow metal accessories, iron stirrups and spurs attached to half-boots completed the dress.

Artillery Dress

Foot Artillery dressed in turkish blue tailcoat and pants; the collar was crimson with a 2-1/2" exploding bomb embroidered in yellow silk together with numbers 1 to 4 for Brigades and 1 to 5 for standing Companies. Cuffs, bars, lining and piping were likewise crimson; buttons gilt with bomb device. The tailcoat had black lapels with 7 buttonholes trimmed with yellow angular pointed lace, and yellow fringeless epaulettes, double vertical pocket flaps in back skirts with 4 buttoned points each and 2" long bomb coattail clasps. The shako was adorned with a tricolor cockade, crimson pompon, two bands at the extremes of the crown and a double angle in back, an emblem with a set of analogous arms and an eagle above, all of yellow brass (an existing artillery shako shows no brass bands or angles).

Dress of the Mounted Artillery was similar to foot cannoneers, with a coatee instead of tailcoat, a 1-1/2" band around the cuffs and three ½" wide diagonal bands on each arm, pants with antelope skin seat lining, leather boots superimposed with their respective straps, and buckskin color gloves with white gauntlets (PL. IX-b, c). Their saddle was like the Cavalry's, saddle blanket and double holster covers of turkish blue cloth with 2" wide crimson border, saddle roll with crimson edging.

Overcoats were turkish blue for foot gunners with crimson collar and embroidered bombs and unit numbers; mounted gunners wore capes and other minor Cavalry dress items.

Engineers' Dress

Engineers dressed in a turkish blue tailcoat with black collar and lapels, crimson cuffs, bars, lining and piping, a special button design, vertical pocket flaps with a wave and a cord, special coattail clasps and all accessories yellow. Officers carried a special model sword and a cane same as senior Infantry officers. Pants were medium blue with a crimson stripe, the shako without cords topped by a pompon for the Sapper Battalion and a tuft for officers not serving with troops (PL. IX-d). Their overcoat was a grey frock coat.

* Cross belt buckles exist in collections which indicate the Light Infantry Battalions had marks indicating the unit name and/or number.

The Battalion of Invalids of Mexico

This unusual unit wore, as of Oct. 3, 1839, a dark blue tailcoat with sky blue lapels, collar, cuffs and bars, deep red piping and a cipher on collar signifying invalids (left).

By 1840, they wore a turkish blue tailcoat with cuffs of same color, but collar, piping and pants sky blue, infantry shako and yellow accessories (PL. VII-e).

Retirees

Retired army officers used a turkish blue tailcoat with collar and cuffs of same color, piping and buttons white, dark blue plain pants, a bicorn hat without lace or plume but with a silver thread tassel fore-and-aft and a 2" tricolor cockade under a ½" wide lace loop ending in a point with a plain button; regardless of rank, no retired officer could carry a cane.

The First Active Regiment of Mexico

This *Milicia* unit used the uniform of the 5th Regulars until July, 1840 when it changed to the dress of the 1st Regulars.

1841: The Reversal of the Regulations of 1840
11th Infantry & 9th Cavalry

On Dec. 22, the uniform regulations of July 10, 1839, with distinctive colors for each unit were again declared in force for the Regular Army, a little over 16 months later.

However, the tailcoat of the 11th Infantry was changed to white with sky blue lapels, collar and cuffs, deep red cuff bars, piping in opposite colors and sky blue pants with deep red piping, the pants being changed later on June 30 1842 to crimson (PL. XII-d), and the 9th Cavalry received a green tailcoat with crimson lapels, collar, cuffs and bars, white piping, dark blue pants with crimson stripe and green saddle blankets (PL. XII-c).

The Tulancingo Cuirassiers

Jan. 15 saw the creation of this "heavy" cavalry regiment.*

Officers and troopers had two changes of uniform. Off duty and dismounted, officers wore a sky blue tailcoat with crimson collar and cuffs, sky blue pants with crimson stripes at seams, a black bicorn hat, straight sword, silver cartouche box, and boots with spurs. When mounted, they wore a sky blue jacket with crimson collar and cuffs, crimson pants (most likely with sky blue stripes at seams), a yellow metal cuirass with national coat of arms in silver, yellow metal helmet with silver ornaments, horse tail on comb, silver belt and cartridge box, sky blue shabraque edged with silver lace, bridle trimmed with silver.

Troopers, when dismounted, had a sky blue jacket with crimson collar, cuffs and bars, sky blue pants with crimson stripes and boots with spurs; when mounted, a yellow metal cuirass and helmet with white metal ornaments and tail on crest, crimson pants with sky blue stripes, black seat lining and half-boots. Their shabraque was sky blue with white band around and their arms were a straight sword with yellow metal grip especially designed for them, and a musketoon (PL. XIII-c).

The Grenadier Guards

On Dec. 7th, a Militia Battalion was organized in the capital and named Grenadier Guards of the Supreme Powers with a strength of 1,200 men in 8 Companies, each with a Captain, 4 Lieutenants., 5 Sergeants., 2 drummers, 1 bugler, 12 Corporals and the rest privates; the HQ Staff had a Colonel, a Lieutenant Colonel, 3 Adjutants, an Armorer, Surgeon, Chaplain, Drum Major and Bugle Corporal.

The Guard was dressed in fine cloth, patent leather belts and straps and bearskin caps 20" high, turkish blue tailcoats with sky blue collars trimmed with black arabesques, black cuffs with double vertical flashes, yellow lace trimmed buttonholes, plain dark blue pants and a brass shield with unit designation at

---

*Despite the official designation as "Heavy Cavalry," and issue of the cuirass, it is probably a mistake to imagine this unit resembling their counterparts in Continental Armies except in name only. Mexican horses were generally much smaller than North American or European mounts, and it is not even certain that the cuirass was actually worn into battle, though one might think that Santa Anna—"The Napoleon of the West"—would have preferred it so!

the crossing of the shoulder belts (PL. XII-a). Half of its officer corps was drained from the Regular Army, and the rank-and-file were contributed by 8 Departments at 150 head each "...All of the same height 5-1/2 ft Mexican and not a sixteenth of an inch less...."

On Sept. 9th, 1842, the Grenadier uniform was changed to a deep red tailcoat with sky blue collar, cuffs and bars, white piping, white lapels with 8 yellow lace trimmed buttonholes, double yellow flashes on cuffs and yellow fringeless epaulettes; pocket flaps were vertical with 3 tassels and an embroidered grenade clasp on each coattail; sky blue pants had yellow piping and the headgear was a fur cap with a brass grenade as shield thus abolishing the Grenadier Guard uniform of Dec. 7th,1841 (PL. XII-b).

1842

On Jan. 17, Auxiliary Cavalry Companies were ordered raised by State governors, remaining under their command in peace but under military authority in armed actions. Governors were authorized to use State funds to buy arms and ammunition or decide arbitrarily on any other way of raising the required amount.

Rural Cavalry Companies were organized on the principal ranch properties under authority of their owners who had to buy arms and equipment from their own funds because their security benefited by this force. Governors and ranch owners had the right to appoint Company officers.

The abuses became so widespread that these Companies were ordered abolished five months later, June 23, except in the Frontier Departments.

Jan. 28, two *presidios* were established along the Mexico-Vera Cruz road for prisoners detailed to road construction.

The supply situation continued uneven. Frequent requests and complaints by field commanders to the War Office furnish proof that dress and equipment of field forces seldom conformed to regulations.

On Feb. 7, General Ciriaco Vazquez reported from his field quarters in Jalapa to the Departmental Treasury in Vera Cruz that "... Black velveteen had to be used because Querétaro cloth can absolutely not be found in the city, and they could not be made of sailcloth either which is still short... all that was available of good quality was taken for the manufacture of another thousand uniforms for units of this g garrison...." Feb. 15, the same General reported that "...The greater part of the rank-and-file of the 2nd Active Battalion, 7th Regular Regiment are short of overcoats, blankets or any other heavier garment that could serve them as cover on rainy and cold nights or when asleep in their quarters, it being necessary for them to go to sleep dressed, with the result that the only uniform issue they possess is quickly destroyed. To avoid this damage and to provide them with an indispensable garment that will make their service more bearable... have the kindness to inform His Excellency the President about the great necessity of providing them at least with one burlap blanket each."

And again on May 7 and 10, General Vazquez ordered to charge every unit with the cost of a canvas uniform by submitting immediately an estimate for a shirt, jacket, necktie, pants and barracks cap in view of the fact that it was impossible to obtain the regulation issue of one cloth and two canvas uniforms, overcoat, blankets, shakos, cloth caps and leather or canvas knapsacks, warning the Treasury that "...His Excellency desires that the units of his command shine not only by their discipline and training, but also by their equipment." On Aug. 14, 1,900 complete canvas uniforms were received from an O'Sullivan contract, including burlap blankets, visored caps, shoulder straps and burlap girdle or scarf.

On June 8, all Accounting Officers were to be dressed up in dark blue tailcoats with low, deep red collar, cuffs and lining, square coattails with 1" wide gold embroidery as per Nov. 25, 1822, around edge of coat, pocket flaps, collar and 2 rows on cuffs, gilt eagle buttons, white cloth pants, short sword and cane, black bicorn hat without plume but with tricolor cockade, gold loop and tassels. The same dress with some differences in embroidery was worn by Intendents, Orderly and War Commissioners, Treasurers and Departmental Accountants; subalterns wore the same items with silver embroidery 4 lines (1/4") wide, and those of Artillery and Navy gold in addition to grenade or anchor device on buttons.

Military Justice Magistrates appeared in straight tailcoat and vest buttoned up to the neck, black pants and low boots, white tie and gloves, bicorn with black plume around, gold loop and gilt button with national arms; they wore around the neck a 1-1/2" white band with circular white enamel shield bearing coat of arms in center and *Departmental Magistrate* lettered around the edge, red enamel border with 3 larger and 3 smaller angular points tipped with green stones, a black gold tipped cane with black tassel and a short sword with gilt grip and justice emblem engraved on guard.

Justice Assessors of Artillery, Engineers, Reserves and Navy wore the March 27, 1837, dress of Lettered Judge without the sash.

On July 5th, officers of the HQ Corps and of the QM Office received a picturesque new uniform with a deep red tailcoat, black velvet collar, lapels, cuffs and bars, piping of opposite colors and collar and cuffs edged with a wide gold lace; on lapels, staff officers had 8 buttonholes embroidered in metallic gold, while subalterns used 5-strand ferret lace with 8 plain buttons, vertical pocket flaps with 3 buttons and eagle coattail clasps. Pants were dark blue with gold piping at seams. The bicorn hat with tricolor cockade was worn by them exclusively on all occasions, with a ½" gold lace edging and tricolor plume for senior officers. The sword-saber worn on a belt under the tailcoat had a green sword knot and black slings. This abolished the Nov. 12, 1835, order; from Aug. 3rd on, HQ Corps subalterns wore the same embroidery as QM Corps staff officers. In 1844, this dress was reformed by substituting white lapels, collar, cuffs and lining and remained in this form until after the war of 1847 (PL. XIII-a).

Beginning Sept. 1st, harbors were guarded by Veteran Infantry Coastguard Companies in dark blue tailcoat with deep red collar, cuffs, bars and piping, dark blue arabesques, Company name or initial embroidered on collar, plain gilt buttons and white canvas pants, all other items according to June 22, 1825, regulations.

On the ordinance end, the government powder mill reported to have elaborated 356 hundredweights or 35,650 lbs of superfine powder for riflemen, 84,150 lbs fine rifle powder, 34,050 lbs medium fine cannon powder and 166,450 coarse miner's powder.

7th Cavalry

On Sept. 10, the July, 1839, uniform of the 7th regular Cavalry was changed to crimson tailcoat with green collar, lapels, cuffs and bars, 8 white lace trimmed buttonholes, piping in opposite colors, green pants with crimson stripe and sky blue saddle blanket with a white band (PL. XIII-d).

Marines

On Sept. 19 a new Marine Infantry uniform was created in a violent color combination of dark green tailcoat, collar and cuffs of the same shade, a 2" yellow silk anchor embroidered on collar, crimson lapels with 9 buttonholes with pointed yellow lace trim, yellow epaulettes, straight perpendicular pocket flaps with crimson piping and yellow lace trim, yellow cuff bars, gilt anchor buttons, two crimson silk embroidered 2" anchors as coattail clasps, around each cuff two yellow lace 1" wide and on each sleeve 3 diagonal yellow flashes; pants were crimson with yellow piping at seams, the shako lined with crimson cloth, an anchor emblem, chinstrap and top and bottom cinch bands as well as 3 angles in back all of yellow metal, a tricolor cockade under a metal loop, a worsted yellow pompon with green streamer, a yellow worsted safety cord attached to the top cinch band. Officers wore the same dress but of finer material and gold lace or embroidery for all that was silk in the rank-and-file dress (PL. XII-e).

The "Fixed" Units

The Standing ("Fixed") Battalion of the Californians that existed from Jan. 19, 1842, to Dec. 1847 wore dark blue tailcoats with red collar, cuffs and bars, piping in opposite colors, initials "FC" (*Fijo de California*) embroidered on collar, yellow accessories, dark blue pants with red piping, shako with brass chinstrap and cinch band.

Up to 1842, Militia uniforms were identical with the Regular Army, but April 18 and 27 of 1842 they received dark blue tailcoats with red collar, lapels, cuffs and bars, yellow piping, yellow metal buttons with unit number or initial stamped on them, sky blue pants with red piping and ornamented shako with red pompon.

The original 8 Standing Companies of 1826 were reduced to two by 1847, their uniform as of Sept. 1842 being a dark blue tailcoat with red collar, cuffs, bars and piping, dark blue arabesques, Company initials embroidered on collar, and white pants for all.

1843

Between April and September, the Grenadiers, Hussars, Cuirassiers and the Light Cavalry Regiment of Mexico were incorporated into the Regular Army.

On September 27, a distinction was provided for officers and men who had lost a limb of their body in defense of national independence. Officers from Sub-lieutenant to General wore on the left breast of their tailcoat a sky blue shield surrounded by a gold embroidered laurel wreath with the name of the invalid and the battle in which he was crippled inscribed on the shield. Sentries presented arms whenever a wearer of this emblem passed. Rank-and-file wore the same shield embroidered in yellow silk instead of gold and sentries shouldered arms when one of them passed, while others of his class had to salute him marching past.

By order of Sept. 28, the standard uniform of Aug. 31, 1840, was henceforth to be worn by Regular Army units only. Retired and Auxiliary Reserve officers had to wear a dark blue tailcoat with red collar, cuffs and piping, yellow buttons and accessories, dark blue pants with red piping at seams, bicorn hat without edging, lace or plume but with a 2" cockade under a ½" wide pointed gold lace loop with plain button, and gold thread tassels at the fore and aft points.

The Jalisco Lancers

On July 19, two Squadrons of Jalisco Lancers were raised, a picturesque unit dressed in a deep red coatee with dark green collar, cuffs and bars, piping opposite, dark blue pants with red stripe, a square topped bonnet with yellow metal shield and yellow cords*, the saddle blanket and holsters green, edged with white band, the saddle roll green with red cover, belts and sword knot of white buckskin (PL. XIII-e).

The Mounted Rifles (*Cazadores*)

On Sept. 20, a unit of Mounted Rifles, originally raised June 12, 1840 as Light Cavalry, were given a new dress consisting of dark green jacket, white piping, crimson collar cuffs, bars and lapels with 12 buttons trimmed with white lace for troopers and silver for officers; they wore a fur busby with yellow metal shield and chinstrap, crimson bag and plume, grey pants with crimson stripes and boots over pants; their cape was yellow, saddle blanket, holsters and roll green with crimson bands around (PL. XIV-c).

The Standing Battalion of Mexico

Sept. 27, a former replacement unit was converted into the Regular Standing Battalion of Mexico and dressed in a white tailcoat without lapels, green collar, cuffs and bars, red piping, plain yellow buttons, 2" high unit initials gold embroidered on collar, vertical pocket flaps with 3 buttoned points, crossed quiver tailcoat clasps and sky blue pants with deep red stripe at seams. The shako had a cinch band, cockade loop and scaled chinstrap of yellow metal, a 2" round tricolor cockade over a yellow metal emblem with national coat of arms and unit initials, all accessories yellow, epaulettes green, pompon green for the 6 Fusilier Companies, with red top for Grenadier and white top for Rifle Company.

The Companies had the usual 80 privates including, whenever possible, a tailor, carpenter, blacksmith, bricklayer, shoemaker and baker; in Company command were a Captain, a Lieutenant, 2 Sub-lieutenants, one First and 4 Second Sergeants, and 9 Corporals. Each Fusilier Company had a drummer, bugler and fifer, the Grenadier Company 4 drummers, buglers and fifers, and the Rifle Company 4 buglers only.

Hussars of the Guard

On Dec. 19, The Hussars of the Guard of the Supreme Powers received their distinctive uniform

---

*The reader will note that the text here, and illustration "e" on PL. XIII, are at variance with the description of the Lancer's Helmet on page 26. However, the latter describes an "Officer's Helmet," and is more in accord with a color photo of the same helmet belonging to the National Museum of Mexico, Mexico City, appearing in *The Mexican War*, by David Nevin, Time Life Books, 1978.

consisting of a fur busby with red bag, a 3 yard long white safety cord and a shield with unit name stamped on it, a deep red dolman without piping but with white cord Brandenburg's and a white stripe down the center, ice blue collar and cuffs edged with white lace and spherical white metal buttons (probably 4 rows of 12); an ice blue pelisse without piping but with white cord Brandenburg's, black fur collar, cuffs and edging, a white suspension cord with a slide button and two flounders at the left side; ice blue pants with white stripe at seams, black leather half-boots and sabretache suspended on 2 slings from a waist belt; red cloth saddle blanket and holster covers with white band around and double bands on holsters; an ice blue cylindrical cloth saddle roll with bands around cover and sides.

This colorful unit was originally a Light Cavalry Squadron transformed on Dec. 8, 1841, from a Public Security Squadron. On Sept. 1, 1843, they were designated an elite troop and rode at the head of all Cavalry formations but were not formally called Hussars until July 27, 1846, retaining this title to January 1848. During the war they served as the Presidential Bodyguard, carrying lances with long red-blue or red pennons (PL. XIII-b).

1845
1st Cavalry

On Sept 7, a distinctive uniform was assigned to the First Cavalry Regiment known in 1837 as the Tampico and in July 1839 as the Number One, consisting of a short dark green jacket with collar and cuffs of the same color, cuff bars, lapels and piping yellow, dark green epaulettes with deep red fringe, white metal buttons, a black helmet with visor, chinstrap and rim of yellow metal, a horse-mane tail and a deep red plume at left side; grey pants with black seat lining, leather half-boots and red stripes at seams; saddle blanket and holster covers deep red with white band around, saddle roll green with deep red cover, white band and circular sides with unit number; their cape was dark blue with green collar (PL. XVI-g).

1846
4th Light Infantry

On March 30, the 4th Light Infantry Battalion was raised and given a uniform considerably different from the other three Light Infantry Regiments, namely a dark blue tailcoat with green collar, piping and arabesques, crimson lapels, cuffs and bars, eagle clasps at coattail turn backs, medium blue pants with crimson piping and white canvas pants for summer (PL. XVI-a).

1847

This last and most disastrous year of the decade left few military dispositions of importance on record.

The behavior of the common soldier and the officers' corps generally was, except in moments of panic and confusion, manly and valorous and on various occasions reached heroic levels. The battles of Angostura, Padierna, Molino del Rey, Churubusco and Chapultepec, studied impartially, assume epic proportions comparable to many of the celebrated major actions of the 19th century.

On Feb. 22, 1847, at Angostura (Buena Vista), Mexican columns made a forced march of 48 miles without a rest before going into battle in steep, broken terrain against U.S. batteries on every hilltop, Infantry and Cavalry well deployed and supplied. Mexican Light Infantry captured the first ridge that night in pouring rain, held it all night without camp fires or food, rifles loaded, protecting the powder pans with their bodies; at the break of day Feb. 23 they again joined battle without breakfast but with boldness, occupying the next line of hills at bayonet point, then the third and fourth one, capturing flags and cannon, while Mexican Cavalry kept charging stubbornly and pierced all American positions.

Having won a legendary battle, they were ordered to fall back 10 miles, abandoning hundreds of wounded. At dawn of the next day, the roll call revealed 3,500 men missing, but within a few hours, the remnants of Hussars, Cuirassiers, Lancers, Dragoons, Sappers, Grenadiers and Light Infantry stood again in battle order, all clamoring to get back into the fight; instead, they received another order to retreat. After 40 days of brutal combats and incessant marches and countermarches, with over 10,000 casualties in dead and wounded, the survivors reached San Luis Potosí on March 9th. Here, they were given 4 days of rest

A. Mexican Army Seal for Defenders of the Valley of Mexico
B. Left Sleeve Emblem
C. Chapultepec Cross
D. Angostura Cross

and sent to stem the American naval invasion of Vera Cruz.

The decimated veterans of Angostura captured Padierna Hill in a bayonet charge and held out to the last man in the hope of reinforcements. At Churubusco, some 600 Volunteers—among them the recently mutinous Bravo and Independence Battalions, city people of the middle class, poorly trained, inadequately armed with inadequate munitions— dug in to block the way of the victorious American columns. At this spot, too, units of the St. Patrick Volunteers (*San Patricios*) made their last stand. This tiny garrison caused 1,016 U.S. casualties and fired off the last available bullet before capitulating.

At Molino del Rey and Casa Mata, the common soldier won the fight but again heard the by now monotonous "orders to fall back."

On his final retreat through rain and mud, carrying his wounded with him on improvised stretchers, followed by a caravan of soldier-women with their pots and kids, the Mexican soldier could look back on 120 months of fighting against Texans, Frenchmen, Americans and against hostile factions of his own fellow citizens; 120 months with 23 changes in government, roughly a different government and command every 5 months.

The years of warfare had brought only tragedy and loss, although the man and the officer in the firing line had borne the burden of sacrifices with unbowed head, and had discharged well their duty to the tricolor flag. Already at the battle of the Alamo, three officers of the 7th and one of the Sapper Battalions died in the attempt to plant the Mexican flag on the rampart, until a Sapper Lieutenant, his name lost in the records, succeeded.

At Palo Alto, not a single color bearer remained alive; the 4th Infantry Battalion alone lost three color bearers in a row. During the bombardment of Vera Cruz, March 1847, a naval Lieutenant and 15 year old Sub-lieutenant three times replaced the Mexican flag shot down during the barrage.

On the tragedy filled 13th of September 1847, the San Blas Battalion left nearly all officers and men as casualties on Chapultepec Hill and its Colonel Xicotencatl, with a deadly wound, managed to salvage the Battalion Colors before he died.

Subaltern Suazo of the Mina Battalion, dying under fire, tried to save the flag by wrapping it around himself before it fell, bloodstained, into American hands. A similar gesture is ascribed to Cadet Escutia.

At Barranca Seca an anonymous sergeant blew up an ammunition box, his flag and himself to prevent them from being captured.

Sergeant Pineda, an 80 year old veteran of the War of Independence, distributed ammunition to the combatants in the firing line at the defense of Churubusco, and Sergeant Navarro, his right arm amputated, kept on encouraging his three sons and was showing them, at the height of the battle, how to load faster. Many pages could be filled with similar manly deeds.

Above the wreckage of these battlefields, behind the haze of a century of neglect by history, there still looms silent and dignified, the ghost of the common Mexican solder of the years 1837-1847.

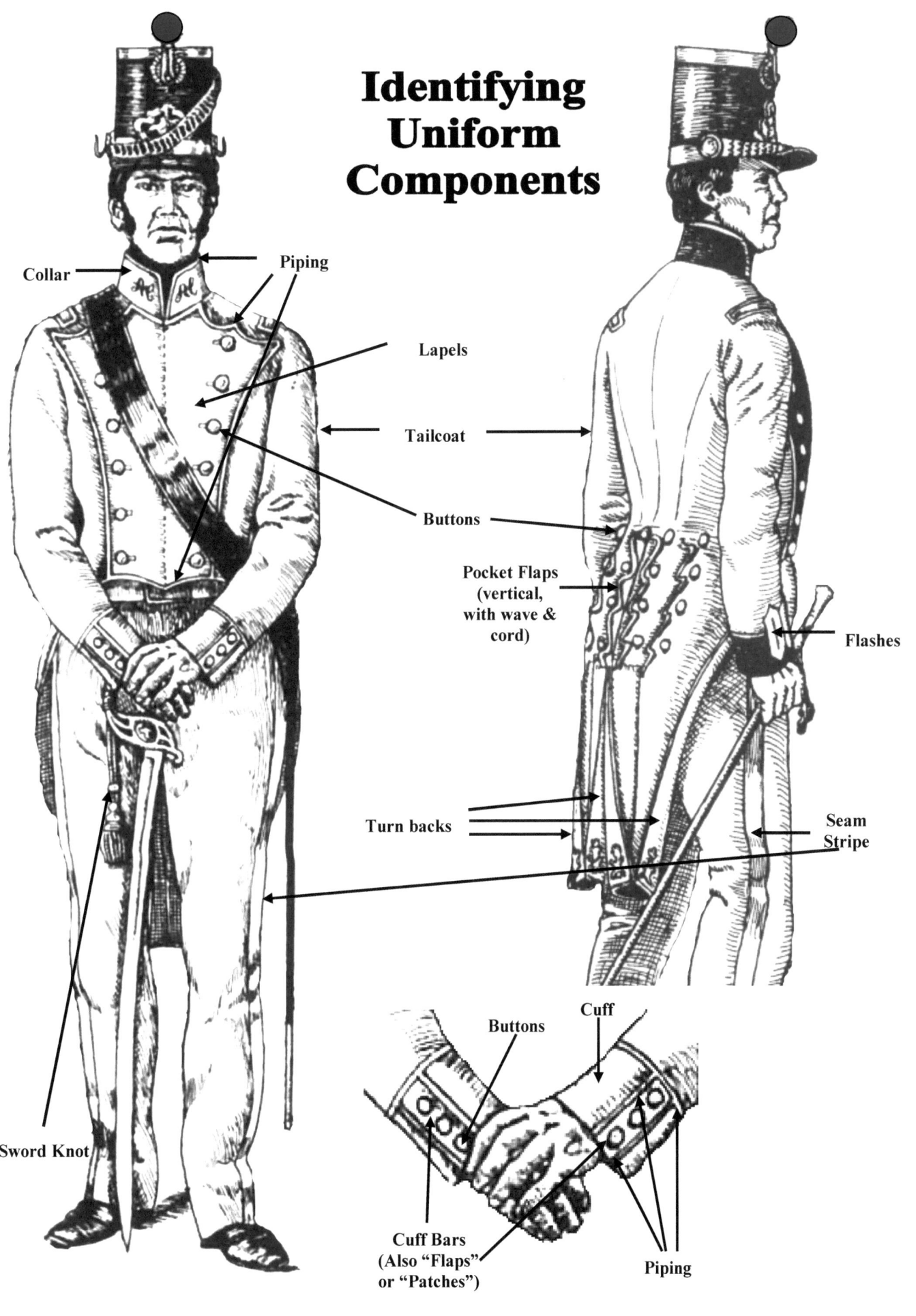

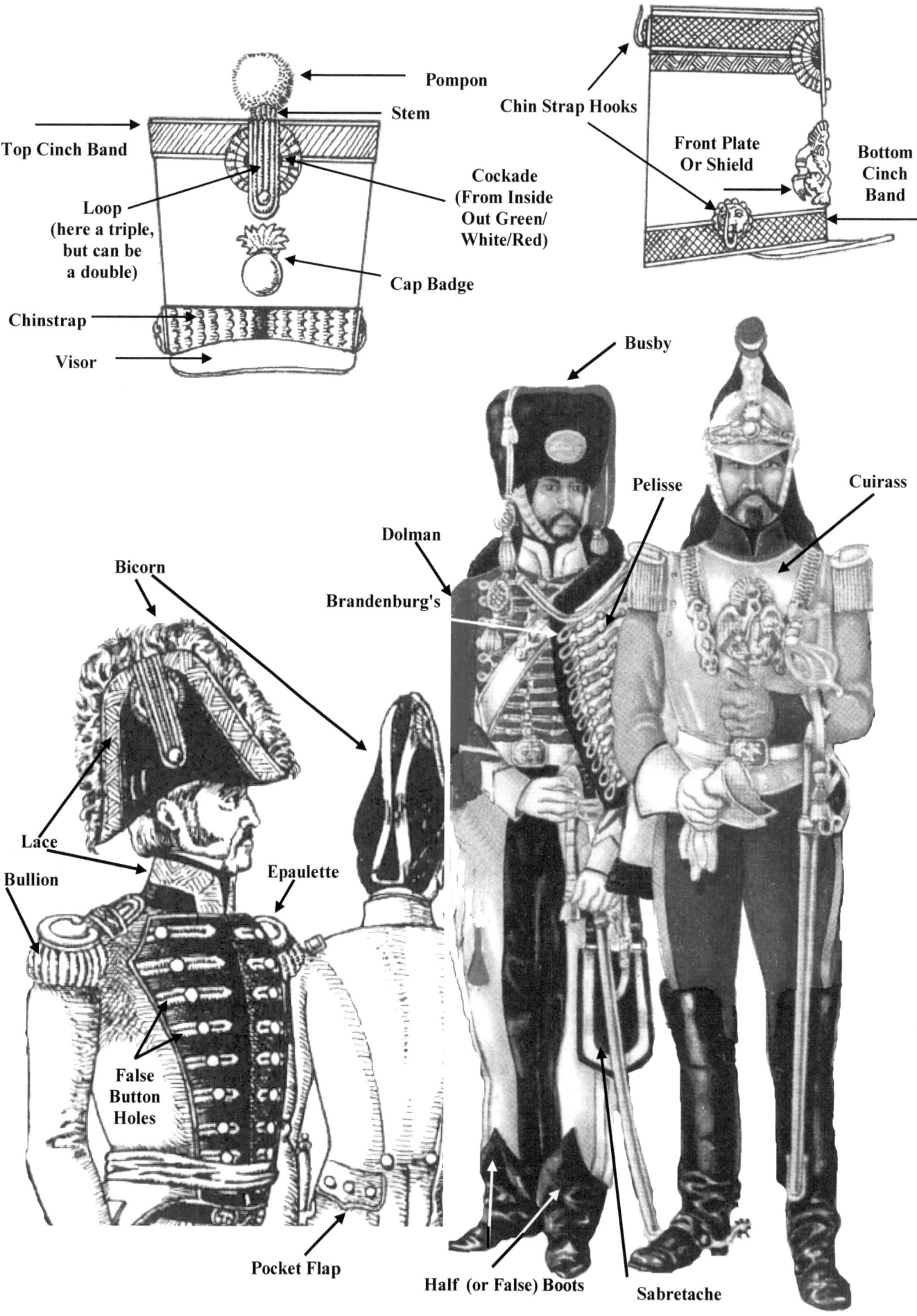

Battle Record of The Mexican Army, 1846-47

Unit ("X" = Engaged)	Palo Alto/ Resaca de Guerrero	Monterey	Angostura/ Buena Vista	Vera Cruz	Cerro Gordo	Valle de Mexico	Padierna/ Contreras	Churubusco	Molino Del Rey	Chapultepec
1st Infantry	X	X	X			X	X*	X	X†	X [1]
2nd Infantry				X						
3rd Infantry		X	X		X†					
4th Infantry	X	X	X		X†				X	
5th Infantry			X		X					
6th Infantry	X				X†					
7th Infantry										
8th Infantry				X						
9th Infantry										
10th Infantry	X	X	X			X	X		X	X†
11th Infantry			X		X	X		X	X	
12th Infantry			X			X	X*		X	X
1st Light Infantry			X		X	X	X	X	X	X
2nd Light Infantry	X	X	X		X	X		X	X	X
3rd Light Infantry		X	X	X	X	X	X	X	X	
4th Light Infantry		X	X		X	X	X	X	X	
Grenadiers of The Supreme Power					X	X				X
National Guard Battalion San Blas						X				X†
National Guard Battalion "Bravos"						X		X		
National Guard Battalion Independencia						X		X		
Cadets of the Military College										X
Active Regiment of Puebla	X		X	X	X†					
1st Active Regiment of Mexico		X	X			X				
2nd Active Regiment of Mexico			X							
1st Active Battalion of Celaya			X			X	X			
Fixed Battalion of Mexico			X			X	X		X	X
Coast Guard Battalion of Tampico			X		X†	X	X			
1st Active Battalions of Guanajuato			X			X	X†			
2nd Active Battalion of Guanajuato			X							
Saint Patrick Volunteers			X		X	X		X		

Battle Record of The Mexican Army, 1846-47

Unit ("X" = Engaged)	Palo Alto/ Resaca de Guerrero	Monterey	Angostura/ Buena Vista	Vera Cruz	Cerro Gordo	Valle de Mexico	Padierna/ Contreras	Churubusco	Molino Del Rey	Chapultepec
Zapadores	X	X	X	X		X	X			
Invalids Battalion of Mexico						X				
1st Regular Cavalry	X	X	X							
2nd Regular Cavalry					X	X	X	X		
3rd Regular Cavalry		X	X		X	X	X	X		
4th Regular Cavalry										
5th Regular Cavalry			X		X	X				
6th Regular Cavalry										
7th Regular Cavalry	X	X	X			X	X	X		
8th Regular Cavalry	X	X	X			X	X	X		
9th Regular Cavalry			X		X	X		X		
Hussars of the Guard			X		X	X	X	X		
Mounted Rifles (Cazadores)			X							
Tulancingo Cuirassiers			X		X	X		X		
Light Cavalry Regiment of Mexico	X	X	X		X					
Jalisco Lancers		X	X							
Active Cavalry Regiment of Guanajuato		X	X			X	X	X		
Active Cavalry Regiment of San Luis Potosi		X	X			X	X	X		
Active Cavalry Regiment of Michoacán & Oaxaca			X			X				
Cavalry of Oaxaca					X					
Light Squadron of Puebla										
Army Medical Corps	X	X	X	X	X	X	X	X	X	X

*Unit was Decimated   † Unit was Wiped Out

X [1] =Though Hefter indicated this unit as "Wiped Out" at Molino Del Rey, other sources indicate at least elements were still engaged at the defense of Chapultepec.

Where a given unit is indicated as "Engaged" at any action, not all Companies were necessarily present: Frequently only Detachments were represented.

This list, though basically correct, is hardly exhaustive. Mexican records became badly confused during and after the war, and *exact* OB's for some actions (notably Buena Vista/Angostura) may not be possible to recreate. Only the units the Author included on his list appear here, though commonly, many more *Guardia Nacional* and *Activo* Battalions, plus independent Companies and Batteries were present at each battle.

Chronology of Government Changes, 1836-48

President	Term In Office
Corro	Feb 27, 1836—April 19, 1837
Bustamante	April 19, 1837—March 18, 1839
Santa Anna	March 18, 1839—July 10, 1839
Bravo	July 10, 1839—July 17, 1839
Bustamante	July 17, 1839—September 22, 1841
Echeverría	September 22, 1841—October 3, 1841
Santa Anna	October 10, 1841—October 26, 1842
Bravo	October 26, 1842—March 5, 1843
Santa Anna	March 5, 1843—October 4, 1843
Canalizo	October 4, 1843—June 4, 1844
Santa Anna	June 4, 1844—September 12, 1844
Herrera	September 12, 1844—September 21, 1844
Canalizo	September 21, 1844—December 6, 1844
Herrera	December 6, 1844—December 30, 1845
Paredes	January 4, 1846—July 28, 1846
Bravo	July 28, 1846—August 4, 1846
Salas	August 5, 1846—December 24, 1846
Farias	December 24, 1846—March 21, 1847
Santa Anna	March 22, 1847—April 1, 1847
Anaya	April 1, 1847—May 20, 1847
Santa Anna	May 20, 1847—September 16, 1847
Peña	September 20, 1847—November 14, 1847
Anaya	November 14, 1847—January 8, 1848

This book, a modest memorial to Mexican Military Tradition, is dedicated to the anonymous soldiers of Mexico—those who have fought, suffered, and died for their country in the centuries past—and those who are serving her in our own days.

Roll of Honor

To The Dons, Caballeros, and Soldados-- of All Nations--Whose Support Made The Return of This Work Possible--VIVA!

(In Order Of Enlistment)

- Dan Schorr
- William G. Armintrout
- Ben Checota
- John Buck
- Russ Haynes
- Michael Curtis
- Robert J. Hanson
- Mark Stevens
- Mike Taber
- Christopher Hughes
- Gary Bitters
- Matt Irsik
- Andrew Robinson
- Allen E. Curtis
- John E. McConnell
- Stephen Chin-Quee
- Daniel W. Groves
- Paul B. Petroff
- Doug Carroccio
- Joseph A. Gepfert
- Brian Weathersby
- Thomas Diener
- Bryan Broocks
- Mark Dolive
- Scott Clark
- William Moreno
- Ross W. Maker
- Steven W. Popper
- Mark Coolidge
- Steve Green
- Tim Herrmann
- Michael A. Borges
- Adrian Stubbs, UK
- Ernesto Rodriguez
- Ector Aguilar
- Robert Burke
- Robert Minadeo
- Anthony A. Noble
- Joshua Bird
- Michael Hazzard
- Tongar E.
- Richard Brooks
- David Tulloch, UK
- Dion Duran
- Timothy Peterson, Canada
- Ken Skinner
- Michael O'Brien
- Uwe Juergen Wild, Germany
- Larry Stehle
- Dermot Odoherty, UK
- Eric Starnes, Poland
- Andrew Kershaw, UK
- Paul Atkin, UK
- Ray Frandsen
- Tony Rocha
- Mike Gindling
- Scott Robertson, Australia
- Michael Zeiler
- Martin Vasquez
- Steven Staniforth
- Ron Vaughn
- Shane Pinkston
- Bill Braham, UK
- Chris & Fred Fischer
- Simon Walker, UK
- Joe Rosendo
- Mitch Brown
- Dannie B. Fogleman
- John Navarro
- Donald Phillips
- Charles Lara
- John Mumby
- Mike Broadbent, Australia
- Nick Futter, UK
- Christopher Scott, UK
- Gary Williams, UK
- John Lawrence
- Rich Low
- Douglas Pappert
- Dave Burt
- Warren Smith
- Mark Chandler, Australia
- Chris Johnson
- Joseph P. Cairo
- Mark Ryan
- Joe Shaughnessy
- Phillip DeLaPena
- J.E. Sansing
- R.M. "Bob" Benavides
- John T. Coleman
- Charles Rivers, Australia
- Roger Dospil
- Joseph V. Rakus
- David Stokes
- Douglass Miller

THE MEXICAN WAR FLAGS COLLECTION
Flags & Standards For The Mexican American War, 1846-48

As part of TVAG's going development of the war game rules for the Mexican War, 1846-48, ***Gone To See The Elephant***, this definitive Collection of Colors, Standards, Guidons and Pennants for the Mexican and US Armies was an early priority. With the help of researchers in Mexico and the US, information and materials on military Colors and Standards were assembled for the first time.

With a constant obsession for detail and accuracy, hundreds of working hours were devoted to designing over 300 Mexican and North American Flags in precise detail. Each is based on existing contemporary examples, the US Army Regulations of 1841, or informed conjecture using the surviving evidence. Now, Colors and Standards for **all** units which fought in the War have been completed and are offered in the two most common game scales, 15mm and 25/28mm.

Printed on high quality paper, the fine detail of these highly accurate flags will be the perfect complement to even the finest painted figures, either for gaming or display.

There are seven separate Flag Sets comprising the Collection. The Mexicans are available in three Sets, the US in four. The Collection consists of between 300 and 325+ flags (depending on specific scale), and sell for $15.00 per Set, except where noted, plus postage.

Set #1: Mexican *Permanente* and *Activo* Infantry Battalions (approximately 50)
Set #2: Mexican *Guardia Nacional* and Cavalry (approximately 50)
Set #3: Mexican Special Addendum—4 sets (12 total) of newly added Infantry and Cavalry flags—$10.00
Set #4: US Regular Infantry & Voltigeurs (44 Flags, both Regimental and National Colors)
Set #5: US Dragoons & Mounted Infantry (45 Flags, with Regimental Standards and Guidons)
Set #6: US Artillery (48 Flags, Regimental and National Colors, and individual Battery Guidons)
Set #7: US Volunteer Formations (68+ 28mm Flags, 80+ 15mm, including Infantry Colors and Cavalry and Artillery Standards)

If bought as single Sets, the cost would be $100.00, but when bought as "The Whole Enchilada," the Discount Price is $60.00.

For full details and to place orders via the Internet, please visit:
http://www.thevirtualarmchairgeneral.com/347-Mexican%20War%20Flags.html

(Flags illustrated are **not** to scale.)

www.ingramcontent.com/pod-product-compliance
Lightning Source LLC
Chambersburg PA
CBHW041512220426
43661CB00047B/1541